JOHN F. KENNEDY,
AMERICAN

JOHN F. KENNEDY

AMERICAN

BY

CHARLES DOLLEN

ST. PAUL EDITIONS

Library of Congress Catalog Card Number: 64-66105

FOR

PETER THOMAS HUNT

who begun his life a few short weeks before President Kennedy sacrificed his. For Peter and millions of other young Americans, the future will be brighter because there was a President Kennedy.

CONTENTS

Foreword

Many there are who appropriately pay tribute to President John F. Kennedy as a world figure, to his skill in political life, and to his devotion in public service. Many others measure the wide interests of his mind, the swiftness of his resolution, the power of his persuasion, the efficiency of his action and the courage of his convictions.

Others recall him as husband and father, surrounded by his young and beloved family. Although the demands of his position carried him often on long journeys and filled even his days at home with endless labors, how often he would take the opportunity to share with his little son and daughter whatever time would be his own. What a precious treasure it is now and will ever be in the memories of two fatherless children. Who among us can ever forget those touching scenes of happy family life which, from time to time, enhanced the elegance of the executive mansion—charming Caroline, jovial "John-John", and at the side of the President, in understanding, devotion and affection, his gracious Jacqueline!

In these pages Father Charles Dollen has captured the flame of youth and promise that burned in John F. Kennedy's life. His was a life of action, full of conflict, excitement, pressure and change;

his was a fully human life, one in which "he lived, felt dawn, saw sunset glow, loved and was loved."

The reader follows John F. Kennedy from the earliest days of his public life, watches him mature with ever expanding responsibility, notes the warmth of his hardy friendship, sees tested under pain and loss the steely strength of his character, joins him in sorrow and joy, in decision and in crises, among friends and with strangers, and measures the qualities of greatness that marked his calm, cool, calculating intelligence and brave, bountiful heart.

Here is a life that we can all ponder with profit in this excellently wrought tribute to: JOHN F. KENNEDY, AMERICAN

JOHN F. KENNEDY,

AMERICAN

I

GROWING UP

Even great men were babies once, and John Fitzgerald Francis Kennedy began life in a happy Boston Catholic home on May 29, 1917. His father, Joseph Patrick Kennedy, Sr., was already at work building the family fortune. His mother, Rose Fitzgerald, was the daughter of a famous politician, who was known far and wide as "Honey" Fitz.

Joseph and Rose had been married by Cardinal O'Connell in 1914. A year later Joseph, Jr., was born, and, since his grandfather had been the first Irish Catholic mayor of Boston, both father and grandfather determined that Joe, Jr. would become the first Irish Catholic president of the United States. Many a proud father has dreamed great things for his first-born, but Joe Kennedy believed that hard work made dreams come true.

Young Jack Kennedy, and the rest of the large family of nine, grew up with this dream fully in mind—Joe, Jr. would some day be president. They all learned, almost from infancy, that ideals and goals were encouraged in this family, but so was the hard work that went into these dreams. Even though the family fortunes went from moderate wealth to great wealth, the children were taught the value of a dollar and the value of the work that went into earning a dollar.

For this was a remarkable family in every sense of the word. The father had to carve his way in the world at a time when Irish Catholics were a noisy minority, sometimes despised, sometimes ignored, and almost always disliked by "society." But Joe Kennedy refused to "know his place," and at twenty-five he became the youngest bank president in the world.

Shortly later, he became assistant manager at the Fore River Shipyard and, therefore, an executive of the Charles Schwab industrial empire. While he was at the shipyard, America began making ships for World War I, and the assistant manager became a close friend of the young Assistant Secretary of the Navy, a man named Franklin Delano Roosevelt.

While Joe Kennedy was working for his family, Rose Kennedy was taking a firm hand in forming the minds and souls of her children. Through her teaching and example, the Catholic faith flourished in the family. Because of her interest, the children were treated to the history and heritage of their faith and their nation.

The Boston area is surrounded with shrines that are sacred to the memory of America's birth and development. Rose Kennedy took the children to visit these places, and every visit was preceded and followed by lengthy discussion about the events that had occurred there. As the children grew, all were encouraged to take part in the discussions.

Dinnertime became a favorite interlude in the day when the father of the family would listen to the results of the historic tours and discussions. Then, current politics, the history of the day, was discussed, and again, the children were encouraged to enter their opinions and defend them. The League of Nations, disarmament, war reparation payments, and all of the exciting events of the 1920's were brought to the attention of all at the dinner table.

Reading was another favorite pastime, fostered by Rose Kennedy. THE NEW YORK TIMES was a favorite newspaper, and its contents were scanned and dissected by all the family. Good books were found in every room. They were well-read and much discussed by the family in the evening. Both Joe and Rose insisted that different sides of important questions be known and considered.

A well-controlled competitive spirit was developed in the Kennedy family through interest in sports. Football, baseball, tennis, golf and water sports were pursued according to the season. The whole family participated and whatever guests were around also had to play. When the family moved to New York in 1926 so that Joe Kennedy could be closer to Wall St., the big worry among the older children was that they would be too far from the water, or that there would be no lawn for "touch" football.

Even the girls became adept at all these sports, and, while they never became "tomboys," they always were able to do their share in family athletic events. Their activities made news even during the presidential campaigns.

Scouting helped develop discipline and control aggressiveness, as did the training in letter-writing. One famous note remains from Jack Kennedy's boyhood when he had to request, in writing, an increase in his 40¢ per week allowance. Actually, money was so little mentioned in the Kennedy household that the children never realized that their father had become a famous multi-millionaire be-

20   JOHN F. KENNEDY, AMERICAN

fore the decade of the 1920's was over, or that he had begun the million dollar trust funds that they would receive later.

As the family fortune continued to grow, the nine children, born between 1915 and 1932, learned to enjoy winter vacations in Palm Beach, summer vacations in Hyannis Port, and the constant travel plans of a big, active family. The children, in order of age, were, Joe, Jr., Jack, Rosemary, Kathleen, Eunice, Patricia, Jean, Robert, and Edward.

Religion was an active force in the Kennedy household, for Rose Kennedy promoted that spirit of joyful Catholicism and confident practice of faith that were to become so famous in her presidential son. Joe, Sr., was away from home more and more in the 1920's and so his influence was more by silent example than by actual teaching.

But Rose performed her task very well. Since much of the formal education of her family was to be in non-Catholic schools, Rose taught the children to live their faith under any and all circumstances. She was insistent that they practice the virtues, rather than argue the Faith. Regularity at Mass and the Sacraments became a normal, natural part of her children's lives.

She made a visit to Church every day, and the pre-school children went with her. Gossip was forbidden in the house, and charity was always the rule. Although they were active youngsters, and they had the usual childhood faults and fights, it was from Rose that they learned to pull together as a family, and to feel a sense of security in each other's loyalty.

The problem of education weighed heavily on her heart. Her husband always felt some resentment at Boston society because he was never fully accepted. He was Irish; he was Catholic. That was enough for the Boston Brahmins, but it was a stimulus to Joe, Sr., enough to make him determined that his sons would never have to undergo this subtle type of persecution.

Joe Kennedy wanted his sons to have the best possible education that America could give them. He was ambitious for his boys and he decided they were to be Americans in every sense of the word. Good Catholic Americans, of course, but he wanted them to meet the right people and be accepted in the best circles. Therefore, he overrode Rose's protests and insisted that the boys attend the best private, secular schools.

The girls could go to Catholic schools—and they did. But Joe, Jr. and Jack were entered in the Dexter School, a private school of the highest standards. Jack went to the first, second and third grades there, only a few blocks from the family home in Brookline, Mass. He left only when the family moved to New York City. Rose loved Boston, and wanted to stay, but everything her husband touched turned to money and it was simply common sense to move to "the big city."

The family settled first in Riverdale, and then in Bronxville, and the search for a school began. Rose looked wistfully for a good Catholic school, but Joe, Sr. chose the world famous Riverdale School. Riverdale had high academic standards and attracted students from all over the world. Since the two boys lived nearby, they were day students.

Jack went through the fourth, fifth and sixth grades at Riverdale, a normal and average young American schoolboy. He received the usual number of average grades and had the usual number of fights. In fact, several of his teachers commented on his quick, hot temper. When this was pointed out to his mother on her frequent visits to the school, she smiled knowingly, for her two older sons often had to be separated from each other at home. The common front that they adopted before outsiders was only equalled by their rivalry between themselves. But Rose Kennedy believed firmly in discipline and knew how to handle these situations.

If John Kennedy's record at school was undistinguished, at least he was remembered for his politeness, his willingness to help, and his bright smile. His first academic interest, even in grammar school, was history, a study that was encouraged by his mother's interest, and aided by his father's questions.

Riverdale School did not go beyond the sixth grade, so it was necessary to find a new school for Jack. Mr. Kennedy yielded to his wife's ideas and had his second son enrolled in Canterbury School, a Catholic boarding school in New Milford, Connecticut. It is staffed with Catholic laymen and has the services of a resident chaplain. Then, as now, its standards are high although its library facilities are small. However, the thirteen-year-old Jack Kennedy would not then have missed the library. Later in his career, libraries were to be a favorite spot for him.

From this point on, the records begin to tell us more about young John Kennedy. This first year away from home gave him a chance to develop as an individual. Away from the influence of his older brother and what seems to have been a favoritism lavished by his father on the older boy, Jack's native independence began to flourish.

For a youngster who was only an average student, at best, his intellectual development really began at Canterbury. The discipline of academic work never fascinated John Kennedy, but he became an omnivorous reader, had a tremendous memory for ideas, and his intellectual ability was far superior to his grades all through his school years.

The teachers at Canterbury encouraged his reading habits, from the Holy Scripture to Ivanhoe, in literature, history and religion. While the boy was absent-minded to the point of carelessness over material things, he treasured ideas and ideals even in these early years. From his mother, by inheritance and training, he had been started on this path. His father added the challenge to excellence and shrewd executive ability. His older brother gave him competition and the growing family of five younger sisters gave him a sense of protectiveness and tenderness. By the time Bobby and Ted were born, Jack was old enough to treasure the thought of more male companionship in the family.

But the one year at Canterbury was certainly providential, even though it was cut short by appendicitis. Later when he was to go to the same school as his older brother, he would never again fall under the spell of Joe's brilliance. He would remain an individual, and both boys learned to respect each other in real fraternal love.

Although he was only a seventh-grader (Canterbury now starts with the ninth grade) Jack was started on Latin. He simply did not like it. When he received 55 on one exam, his teacher felt it necessary to write the boy's parents. We will never know what Joe, Sr. wrote to his son, but Jack applied himself to his Latin studies much more seriously after hearing from his dad. Spelling wasn't a JFK subject either, and all his life the niceties of English spelling held pitfalls for him. The scope of his intelligence was wide and deep. His memory and reading ability were invaluable aids to that intelligence. But he simply had no mind for, or patience with, details.

He seemed to thrive on the religious atmosphere at the school and frequently mentioned it in his letters to his mother. Throughout his life he had a deep, intense faith which showed itself in his actions. From these earliest years he detested making a show of his faith, or a public display of his love of God, but it was all the more real because he "lived" it very fully.

At Canterbury Jack was introduced to organized sports for the first time. He threw himself into the program with real enthusiasm, but football and swimming were his favorites. His swimming prowess was to become almost legendary later during his Navy career, but water sports were a life-long passion with him. During the family vacations, Joe, Sr. hired a professional athletic director to supervise the sports activities of the youngsters. Physical fitness and work-outs were as much a part of the Kennedy way of life as attendance at Mass every Sunday or the love of good books. "A sound mind in a sound body" summed up this aspect of the Kennedy philosophy.

That year when Jack went home for Easter vacation he was well-adjusted to boarding school and looked forward to returning for the full course. But he was stricken with appendicitis and the long recovery kept him from finishing the school year. As it turned out, it was his last year in a Catholic school, for his father decided to send him to Choate where Joe had been for two years.

Choate is a "prep" school of the highest social standing, and while it is nominally a religious

JOHN F. KENNEDY, AMERICAN

oriented school, it is best known for the social elite it serves. Adlai Stevenson and Chester Bowles are graduates of the school. Since Joe, Sr., wanted his boys to move in the best circles, he could hardly have chosen more wisely. However, Rose Kennedy wisely feared the influence of secularism and religious indifference.

She might slip a prayer book or a good religious book into a package she was mailing to him. She didn't have to worry too much, however, for frequently Jack would mention receiving Communion or slipping in to visit Church in the middle of the week. There were few Catholics at Choate, but Jack managed to meet and become friendly with those who were in his own age group.

Again at this new school, John Kennedy did not excel in his studies. The teachers constantly reported to his parents that he was capable of great work but simply wouldn't apply himself. Only in English and history did he do well and that came naturally. At Canterbury, when he was only thirteen, he had asked for a subscription to the LITERARY DIGEST, and at Choate he had a subscription to the NEW YORK TIMES, both of which he read thoroughly.

His spelling remained atrocious and his grasp of foreign languages went hardly beyond the fundamentals. About all that can be said for his Latin was that he learned how to use the subjunctive and not split infinitives. He thought French close to impossible, which helps to explain his genuine delight in later years at Jackie's fluency in the language. He was interested in the sciences but never adept at them. When academic subjects demanded nothing more than a worship of details, John Kennedy lost interest.

To his mother's mortification, Jack's lack of neatness in his room became a subject of many letters from the headmaster. At home, the older children accepted some of the responsibility for the younger children as well as sharing in the usual household chores. But the cold formality of boarding school simply did not inspire Jack to feel personal responsibility for his rooms. If he threw a pair of old jeans across a chair, they would stay there 'til he needed them again! The headmaster thought differently. It is hard to feel too much sympathy for that harassed official, for the boy's rooms sound like a very typical American teen-age boy's room anywhere in the country, when mother isn't around.

Part of the difficulty might have stemmed from Jack's extra-curricular activities. His brother Joe was playing varsity sports and winning scholastic awards, and, with the perversity of some well-meaning teachers, this was constantly being flaunted in Jack's direction. "Your brother does this . . ." "Your brother does that . . ." Fortunately, this never came between the boys themselves, but Jack did turn to other fields in which he might be himself.

One of these activities was the formation of an unusual club. A small handful of the boys, using

the Kennedy room for headquarters, gathered themselves into an illegal group called "Muckers." Their
escapades included leaving the grounds after lights-
out for trips to the local soda shop. While innocent
in itself, no school can allow these things, and
Choate was not about to, either.

When a denunciation in chapel didn't work,
stern letters to parents followed. When Joe, Sr.,
arrived on the scene to hear his son's explanation, the
"Muckers" quickly became past history. Jack's
talents had to be turned to different channels for
the self-expression that his dynamic personality demanded. Intra-mural sports helped use up some of
this energy, even though the coaches would never
consider him for varsity sports. They felt that he
was too slight of build and that he didn't want to
practice hard enough. True, when he was on the
field and in a real game, he was all business, but
coaches are afraid to trust athletes who don't want,
or need, practice drills.

Jack's first personal experience in politics came
during these high school days. In 1932 Roosevelt
was running against Hoover and, as happens in
many schools, a mock election is held to teach the
students the importance of the American political
system. Jack chose to campaign for FDR, his
father's old friend. Since Choate served the families
of old established wealth, for the most part, and
these are usually Republican, it goes without saying that Hoover carried the schoolboy vote better

than four to one. But it was an exhilarating experience for young Kennedy, one that he would never forget.

Jack went through his adolescence at Choate, from frail childhood through the fuzzy-cheeked period to tall handsome young manhood. He learned to dance well and enjoy parties, to acquire social graces and to feel at ease with his well-merited popularity. He fulfilled his father's hopes, for he became a much sought-after member of the social circles that had rejected his dad. He made friendships and contacts that endured all his life. All told, his years at Choate were most profitable for him.

And his mother's fears for his faith were certainly unfounded. If anything his faith grew stronger and deeper during these years. During the "bull sessions" that young men enjoy so much, when they solve so many of the world's problems, Jack was often challenged to explain or defend his beliefs. This sent him to books for explanations and study. He read the papal encyclicals that were issued during those years when Pope Pius XI was at his eloquent best. How many high school boys, even in Catholic schools, read and discuss encyclicals? But John Kennedy always did, a practice he started at Choate.

When he was graduated in 1935, sixty-fourth in a class of one hundred and twelve, no one suspected that a future president had walked down the aisle. His classmates certainly liked him, for they had voted him "most likely to succeed." However this was because of his energy and determination, not because he had been an outstanding student or athlete. More than likely they were considering the family business ventures that could have opened many doors to a determined young man.

But the immediate prospect before him was college, even while the war clouds gathered. The Communists had started "United Front" activities; Hitler had defied the Versailles Treaty; Mussolini had invaded Ethiopia; the persecution of the Jews had begun in Germany, and the depression was still ravaging America. The American Labor Unions had finally won the right to organize for collective bargaining and Social Security was founded. 1935 was certainly an exciting year to begin college for a young man who was very interested in current events and who brought a wide background of historical perspective to strengthen his interests.

2

COLLEGE

Joe Kennedy, Sr., was a staunch capitalist of the rugged American school of finance. When Roosevelt became president, he gave Mr. Kennedy the delicate job of starting the Securities Exchange Commission with the task of regulating the stock market to try to avoid future depressions. This man, who had become a multi-millionaire by speculating in stocks, knew from experience both the strengths and weaknesses of the American system.

But socialists and communists did not want the American economy to grow along capitalistic lines. They wanted to re-make the United States along their ideas. However, Joe Kennedy was the type of man who learned from his own mistakes, and who did not fear to learn from his enemies. He steered a course that was mid-way between the rugged individualism of the nineteenth century and the government-controlled systems of socialism. He was very successful in this course, and he was determined that his sons would learn as he did.

Therefore, in the summer of 1935, he sent young Jack to London to study at the London School of Economics under the brilliant socialist, Harold Laski. Joe Kennedy wanted his sons to rub elbows with radicals and revolutionaries so that they would know, by experience, what to avoid in the fields of politics and economics. And, many of the programs of the socialists had the well-being of the poor and the working man at heart. Mr. Kennedy felt that these modern programs could be adopted by Americans and translated into a free society. Democracy should be able to absorb the best of both worlds, the left and the right, and, in a free world, these programs would really be able to benefit the greatest number of people.

The world of the 1930's was in a ferment over these ideas. Social justice and Christian charity demanded that the working classes be given a fair share for their labor, good working conditions, and security for their families. The encyclicals of Pope Pius XI took up these ideas in a Christian context. Even Father Coughlin gained a following of millions of listeners in America through his radio broadcasts about social conditions from the Shrine of the Little Flower, near Detroit. America wanted, and needed, social progress, and Joe Kennedy wanted his sons to be in the middle of this battle for human rights.

Unfortunately, both Father Coughlin and Joe Kennedy were to be attracted by extremism, as subsequent events proved, but they were making history and were caught up in the need for action. Yet, these years were formative years for eighteen-year-old Jack Kennedy, and they help to explain why, later in life, he was to be so interested in unions, civil rights, and a war on poverty. It also shows us what a progressive turn of mind he would have as president, calling for equal opportunity and full rights for all men, and why the cause of mankind would be close to his heart, whether in West Virginia or West Berlin. It would be no wonder that he and Pope John XXIII saw eye-to-eye in fighting for human rights.

Jack had to return to America because the jaundice that was to plague him all year had begun. His older brother, Joe, Jr., was at Harvard, and Jack decided that he did not want to live in the shadow of a very successful and popular older brother. With much difficulty, he persuaded his father to allow him to go to Princeton where some of his friends from "Mucker" days were going.

The year at Princeton was not a fortunate one, and, in fact, it was never finished. Even before the football season was over, jaundice had returned and Jack had to leave school. He spent most of the winter in Arizona, regaining his health. When he returned to New York, he told his father that he wanted to go to Harvard, a decision that was entirely his own, but one that he knew would please his dad.

Jack's years at Harvard were no more distinguished than his years at Choate had been. He was an average student, an average athlete, and reasonably popular. One of the chief reasons for this was the simple fact that he was so full of life, so vital, so interested in everything. Or to put it another way, because his interests were so broad and universal, he did not concentrate on any one field for excellence. The very success of his older brother, both academic and social, opened many doors for young Jack and allowed him to coast along in reflected glory. He had forseen this and tried to stop it by going to Princeton, but when that had failed and once he was caught up in this, it was only too easy to go along with it.

During his freshman year he was appointed chairman of the Freshman Smoker, a traditional stag party designed to unite the new students and bring them into the social whirl of the campus. It marked Jack as a member of the "social" set on campus, as opposed to the "political" set. For "The Yard," the Harvard Campus, mirrored the world around it, and there were Fascist clubs, Communist cells, socialist groups, and Democratic and Republican activities.

Jack Kennedy kept himself aloof from these groups. He was interested in these activities but already the wide scope of his mind and interests kept him from identifying himself with any of these ardent, earnest, and almost fanatical groups. He was active in the St. Paul Catholic Club, the Hasty Pudding, an exclusive social club, and Spree, an even more exclusive prestige club.

Swimming and sailing remained his first loves among all his extra-curricular activity, and he won an inter-collegiate award for Harvard in sailing. He also made junior varsity football. He went out for most sports, but his tall, thin build did not suit him for a spot on most of the teams. However, he put everything he had into the sport or work at hand, which was characteristic of him. His first serious back injury came in a junior varsity football game.

In his sophomore year, Jack won a place on the CRIMSON, the student paper at Harvard, and this started an interest in journalism that was to last all his life. Once when reporters asked him what he would do when he left the White House, his first response was that he would probably buy a newspaper and work on it. Franklin D. Roosevelt had once been editor of the CRIMSON, a fact which did not escape Jack's notice.

But the world of the late 1930's was rapidly falling apart. Hitler, Mussolini, and Stalin were on the move; Japan was stepping up its war in China; a recession had hit America; Franco was winning his struggle to free Spain from Communism, and Neville Chamberlain returned from Munich promising "peace in our time." In the summer of 1937 Jack Kennedy went to Europe and observed most of these things for himself. From this time on, practical politics ceased to be a matter of reading the NEW YORK TIMES or simple talks at home, and Jack knew, from then on, that this was the world in which he would give his all.

His role as a political analyst began that summer with the letters he wrote home, and while they may have been somewhat naive, they showed the keenness of mind and whole-hearted devotion that would help him become a truly professional politician, once he had more training and experience. That summer he was impressed by Mussolini's efficiency and Britain's need for a stable Spanish government. He recognized that the Spanish Republic had been betrayed by the Communists and that, while Franco must win in order to save Spain, he hoped that democracy would return to Spain, some day.

When John Kennedy returned to Harvard he began to take his political science courses seriously. He had found himself, now, and his studies improved so much, that ultimately he would graduate with honors. Then, he discovered Professor Arthur N. Holcombe, teacher of American government, and this was the turning point in his academic career, for the professor drew from him an energetic and enthusiastic response to politics.

They became fast friends both in and out of the classroom. In class, the professor might assign Jack a term paper on some right-wing Republican politician, and demand a thoroughly objective analysis of the man. Out of class, they might discuss the current day's issue of the CONGRESSIONAL RECORD, or a recent editorial in the TIMES. The brilliant, friendly, and perceptive attitudes of the moderately liberal Arthur Holcombe helped form the political thinking of John Kennedy, teaching him lessons that he would never forget. Both had quick, sympathetic minds; both rejected special pleading from the ultra-conservatives and the ultra-liberals. Both men, teacher and pupil, were dedicated to forward-looking progress in the American way of life.

President Roosevelt had appointed the elder Kennedy to the post of Ambassador to London, and he wanted to share the challenges of this exciting post with his family. Jack took six months off from college and began to work as a courier for his father. His activities centered in London and Paris, but his trips took him to Danzig, Warsaw, Latvia, Russia, Turkey, Jerusalem, the Balkans and the Riviera. The confidential reports that Jack sent back to the London Embassy left no doubt that he was maturing politically. Nor was there any doubt at the keenness and quickness of his mind in gathering and assessing the data he collected.

However, Joe, Sr., had adopted an isolationist policy, an attitude which was popular in America with many people, but unrealistic as far as the world situation went. Mr. Kennedy was close to Neville Chamberlain and the conservatism of the two men blinded them to the fast pace of world politics. The Rome-Berlin Axis seemed invincible, and negotiation seemed the most profitable hope for some sort of peace. The policy of appeasement only stalled off the inevitable—war, or surrender to world Fascism.

War came on September 1, 1939. Hitler had demanded Danzig from Poland, and, as Jack Kennedy had reported to his father months earlier, the Poles rightly refused to bow to Nazi demands. England and France were forced to act, and two days later they declared war on Hitler. Stalin had treacherously concluded a pact with Hitler which allowed Hitler free reign in Central Europe. Jack had warned his father of this posssibility after his trip to Moscow, Leningrad and the Crimea because he had witnessed the Russian hatred of the West and its fear of Germany. Many other commentators had foretold this possibility, too.

Only twelve hours after the outbreak of war, German submarines sank the large passenger vessel, the ATHENIA. Among its fourteen hundred passengers and crew were about three hundred American citizens. The survivors were returned to English and Irish ports, and Jack Kennedy was sent to Glasgow to interview the American citizens. He also had to arrange passage home for them on other ships. When they demanded Naval protection, Jack had to refuse, for the American government had immediately proclaimed neutrality in the European conflict. Ambassador Joe Kennedy had been one of the most insistent advisors in this policy. Again, Jack had to differ with his father, for the clouds of war were obviously gathering over America, too.

Jack hurried back to Harvard to finish his college career before the war should come. By this time he was a millionaire, himself, for his father had settled huge sums of money on each of his children, to insure their independence. Jack had to take extra courses to make up for his leave of absence, but he was determined to obtain his degree before the war engulfed the United States.

He settled down to his most serious school year ever, and he proved to all that when he did apply himself, he was capable of excellent scholastic work. Besides the extra class work, Jack began work on his great controversial thesis which was to be pulished later as a book with the title WHY ENG-LAND SLEPT. It has sold over one hundred thousand copies.

Young John Kennedy had always loved to read, and he had developed an historical sense under his mother's direction, but now he started to haunt the great Harvard Library. While working on his thesis, he learned how to uncover the treasures in a library, how to brief subject lists and use digests. He learned the importance of the Index and Abstract services in order to search out the most dependable works of the best writers. The card catalogue of Harvard's Widener Library, with its millions of cards, became a familiar learning place for him. In all, John Kennedy learned how to do research with all the infinite patience that is required to taste the joys of successfully learning new things.

Jack's thesis was an investigation into the social and political background behind Chamberlain's appeasement policy. Granted the English scene as it actually was, neither Chamberlain nor his predecessor, Baldwin, could be personally blamed for the British weakness. In this, Jack and his father agreed for both men were political realists. The Munich Pact, and the whole idea of giving in little by little to Hitler, actually was an expression of English public opinion.

World War I had been so frightful a calamity that it had destroyed society as Europe of the nineteenth century knew it. The horrors of the economic depression were just as bad, and the English people really wanted peace. The disarmament pacts of the 1920's seemed to be a guarantee to some sort of stability and, when Germany, Italy and Japan began to rearm, the British public stubbornly refused to take it too seriously. As Kennedy saw it, the idea of buying peace at the expense of Austria or parts of Czechoslovakia seemed to the English people a very small sacrifice—especially since Hilter assured the world that that would satisfy him.

Jack wrote, "England so hated the thought of war that she could not believe it was going to happen." He knew that Hitler should have been stopped at his very first act of aggression. And he, personally, learned the lessons of history. Over twenty years later he took a strong stand with Russia in Cuba, and he approached disarmament with cautious hope, obvious of the need for real bilateral action.

Kennedy pointed out that England could not exist in a sort of grand isolationism from the rest of the world. Neither could America. Only future historians will be able to assess the degree of American guilt for not supporting the League of Nations and for turning it back, not only on Europe, but the rest of the world as well.

In the conclusion of his first book, John Kennedy analyzed the strengths and weaknesses of democracy and dictatorship. Since a democracy must serve the interests of its people, it must produce leaders who can reach the people with dynamic ideas and inspire them to act in the cause of justice. What the dictator gains in efficiency he loses in human rights and values and so has nothing of permanent value to leave his people.

Finally he wrote, "It is right and proper to support vigorously our way of living as being the greatest in the world, but it is not right and proper to be blind to its weaknesses." And, "We cannot tell anyone to keep out of our hemisphere unless our armaments AND THE PEOPLE BEHIND THESE ARMAMENTS are prepared to back up the command. . . . We should profit by the lesson of England and make our democracy work."

With these views, Jack was bound to grow further and further away from the views of his father and older brother. As they seemed to become more aggressively isolationist, Jack seemed to realize that democracy itself was on trial all over the world. Joe, Jr., formed a non-intervention club at Harvard Law School, and Joe, Sr. started to give talks around the country on non-involvement in the European fight.

In fact, the Ambassador became so convinced that England couldn't win, that he had a falling out with President Roosevelt. After the election in 1940, in which FDR became the only three-term president of the United States, Mr. Kennedy adopted the America-First cause completely. He had to resign, of course, as Ambassador to London as he found himself in complete opposition to the Democratic party chieftains.

Roosevelt was leading the nation on the only course it could take, a course which was to give America the leadership in the free world. He began by making America the "Arsenal of Democracy," and at the same time, strengthening the United States for its role in World War II. He had powerful opposition on all sides so that the country finally did go to war poorly prepared, but FDR was certainly a belligerent neutral as the 1940's started.

All of this confusion was effective in John Kennedy's life, too. He had graduated from College and had to choose a career. At first he considered Yale's law school, but hesitated about a legal vocation. He knew he didn't want to go to Harvard where his brother Joe was so active. He enrolled in Stanford's business school, and actually went to California to begin classes.

However, when the first semester was over, Jack left school and began a tour of Latin America. This trip lasted several months but when he returned, his mind was made up. He would enter the military to prepare for the war that was about to erupt.

3

THE NAVY

The war in Europe continued to see fresh German conquests, and during 1940 and 1941, the Balkans fell to Hitler, and the march to Moscow began. Although young Joe Kennedy was a confirmed isolationist, he did believe in a strong America. Early in 1941 he decided to finish his second year in law school and then enter the Navy's aviation cadet program.

About this time, Jack returned from South America with his own decision to enter the Army.

To his dismay, he discovered that he could not pass the physical exam. He really wanted to enter the Army Air Force, but he knew that the back injury he had sustained playing football would rule that out. He never thought it would keep him from all military service.

But he wouldn't take "No," for an answer and he began a long series of treatments and physical exercise. Finally, with a little political maneuvering, he was able to pass the Navy's physical. Even then, the best he could do was to obtain a desk job in Washington. He was assigned to the Navy Chief of Staff office as an intelligence officer with the duty of preparing a daily digest of the latest news for the Chief of Staff. While it was a responsible job, it wasn't very exciting for the idealistic young man.

When the Japanese attacked Pearl Harbor on December 7, 1941, Jack could stand it no longer. He mustered up every bit of influence that he, and his father, could manage, and at last received an assignment that offered real challenge. He was sent to the torpedo boat (PT Boat) training school in Melville, Rhode Island. His skill on the water in boats and aquatics qualified him to become an instructor at the station.

He knew many of the men there from his days at Harvard and Princeton and made many additional friends who were to stand by him all his life. Byron White, whom he later appointed to the Supreme Court, and Paul Fay, whom he would name Under-secretary of the Navy, were PT men and associates of his. Torpedo boats were still untried under fire, and while the theory of a small fast boat, capable of packing a punch and moving out, seemed acceptable, the squadrons still had to prove themselves. The boats were beautiful, sleek 70-footers, capable of 40 knots (45 m.p.h.), able to carry and launch the deadly torpedos that cause fear in the heart of any sailor.

Jack was tall and thin, which accounted for his navy nickname, "Shafty." He looked so young that he was often mistaken for a dependent, or a young recruit, to the subsequent embarrassment of many a man who came aboard the station, only to find that he was an instructor. He shared their cocky self-confidence, which turned out to be over-confidence once they were in the South Pacific. But so high was their morale that, under fire, they were able to change their techniques and tactics to become more effective. The most fatal flaw in torpedo boat warfare is the fact that they must operate in silence, depending on surprise and speed for their success. This means that they cannot communicate with each other except visually or by flag. At night or in a fog, this can be extremely dangerous, and almost cost John Kennedy his life later.

After the crews of several squadrons were trained, Jack was sent to a PT Squadron in the Panama Canal Zone and, shortly afterwards, to the Solomon Islands, where some of the most bitter fighting of the entire war was taking place. By this time Jack was a Lieut. (j.g.) and he was given command of the famous PT 109. For a while, maintenance of the boats was the most difficult task that faced the squadron. The crews in the South Pacific had their own theme song, which began:

Oh, some PT's do forty-five,
And some do thirty-nine;
When we get ours to run at all
We think we're doing fine!

And it was necessary to keep their boats at top efficiency, for the Marines, in 1942, were carrying the war to the enemy, and because of their courage and heroism, America finally was beginning to get the taste of victory. In the fall of 1942 the Japanese advance was stopped because the Marines were "fightin' fools" unwilling to be stopped by any challenge. Everything the Navy had was put at the service of the Leathernecks.

From late fall 1942 until February of 1943, the Marines bought every inch of Guadalcanal with the price of their blood. The American nation can never praise too highly the exploits of the Marine Corps, but in the South Pacific, the corps rose to new standards of excellence. For after Guadalcanal it seemed as if every island in the whole region would become an equally bloody battleground. Jack Kennedy never forgot the sight of scarred, battle-weary Marines making landing after landing, facing gunfire bombardment and fanatical suicide charges.

The Navy had to destroy the Imperial fleet to prevent supplies and re-enforcements from coming. Navy and Marine Corps pilots had to battle tremendous odds in the first year and a half of war. In one engagement, sixteen Marine Corps pilots rose to challenge over eighty Japanese planes. With courage like this around them, the PT crews were inspired to take incredible risks to support the Marine Corps actions. While it is doubtful that the PT's actually sank any enemy ships, they caused havoc and frantic activity among the Japanese simply because they were there, and could be so deadly. The torpedo boats ran here and there, close to shore and then out for a close sorty with destroyers, keeping the Japanese fleet tense, nervous, and alert.

The PT's had their last full encounter with the "Tokyo Express" during the night of August 12, 1943. Fifteen boats went out to meet four destroyers that were in the vanguard of the approaching fleet. In the darkness, the boats lost contact with one another, but first one, then another would come into torpedo range of the Japanese ships. The flash of the torpedo launching warned the destroyers in time to change course. As each PT boat fired its four torpedos, it would turn and head for home base and rearmament, and then head back to the battle.

At 2:30 in the morning, the PT 109 made contact with the Japanese. A dark shape loomed up close to the boat; at first the sailors thought it was another PT, but it was on a collision course with them, and, as Lt. Kennedy turned to avoid it, its size became evident. It was the Imperial destroyer Amagiri. Kennedy went into his torpedo-firing pattern, but the darkness and the speed of the two vessels brought them together before he could execute emergency escape.

The Amagiri did not fire at PT 109, nor did it slow down. More than likely, the ship did not even know it had hit a boat at that time, and probably thought that floating debris caused the damage to the destroyer's hull. Even the fire that engulfed the PT 109 did not disclose its presence to the Japanese, and the destroyer's moving full speed probably pulled the flaming gasoline into its wake and saved many lives. Kennedy, and two ensigns, Thom and Ross, started gathering in the survivors, some of whom could not swim, and some of whom were seriously burned.

By dawn, all but two of the crew were gathered back on the floating hulk that had been PT 109. With daylight, the eleven survivors discovered that the boat was slowly taking on water and would soon sink. There was no activity visible on the ocean in any direction, and of the two closest islands, the largest was feared to be unsafe, and the smaller was chosen, even though it meant a swim of close to four miles. Kennedy had already given up his life belt, and the clothes of all the men were torn, ragged, or missing. Jack had to make the swim dressed only in T-shirt and shorts.

A small raft was made for the non-swimmers and they and the poor swimmers were tied to it. What little could be salvaged was placed on it (it was little more than a board), and that included seven pistols, three knives, and one flashlight. The first aid kit had been lost in the collision. They arrived safely on Bird Island, but exhausted, hungry, and practically naked. For the next five days, their diet was to consist almost entirely of cocoanut meat and cocoanut milk.

That evening, Kennedy decided to swim out into Ferguson Passage, a PT boat patrol area, with the hope of sighting a friendly boat. The area was also well-patrolled by Japanese aircraft, and some larger Japanese ships. Jack worked his way from one little islet to another, swimming along reefs and across passageways. While he did not see any PT's, he did observe flares and air activity in the opposite direction, indicating that the patrol activity had taken place in the alternate area of operations. When he attempted the return swim, he was caught in the current that swept through Ferguson Passage at night, and he was taken out to sea. He circled around for almost two miles before returning to his starting point. Then he still had the return swim to Bird Island. He stopped off on a tiny island to sleep and at dawn returned to the rest of his group.

The next night, Ensign Ross volunteered to go out in the opposite direction, but again with negative results. Profiting from his skipper's experience, he hid on an islet during the night to avoid the treacherous current, and returned at dawn. The food supply on Bird Island began to run out, so Kennedy had to move the men to another island.

One man, McMahon, the most seriously injured, had to be towed by Kennedy to their new "home." The others followed slowly, experiencing great difficulties with the changing currents. Although this new island was slightly larger and had more brush for cover from Japanese planes, its supply of cocoanuts proved to be even less than Bird Island. Finally, Kennedy and Ross decided to risk a swim to the large Cross Island, even though there was real danger that it was occupied by the enemy. They had observed New Zealand planes strafing the island which meant that there was suspicious activity on it.

The two men made the swim at dusk and darted into the covering brush. They sighted two figures whom, from lack of trousers, they decided were natives, but they could not attract their attention. Then they came across a large carton with Japanese markings which contained crackers and candy, and finally they found a barrel of water and a one-man canoe. Kennedy took the canoe and proceeded further out into the passage, looking for PT boats. Again he was unsuccessful, so he returned to Ross and picked up the food and water to take back to his men.

When he arrived at the camp, he discovered that the two natives had seen him, and they had circled back until they saw the survivors. Ensign Thom used every bit of ingenuity he could muster to convince the natives that they were not Japs and finally they landed and started to help the Americans. From their knowledge of the terrain, they could prepare foods that the Americans would have been afraid to try. They also applied primitive first aid to the injured men.

The next day, Kennedy and the natives went back to Cross Island, picked up Ross, and began a search for Japanese. They found none, but they did find another, two-man canoe. The natives knew where the Allied Coastwatcher was hidden, so they took messages from Kennedy and Ross to deliver to him. Ross had a small pencil stub and wrote the message on a scrap of paper, but, for fear the natives might get it wet and lose the message, Kennedy took a cocoanut shell and carved out a message:

NAURU ISL.   NATIVE KNOWS POSIT. HE CAN   PILOT.   11 ALIVE.   NEED SMALL   BOAT.   KENNEDY.

The natives left to communicate with the New Zealander who served as coast-watcher in the region. These men lived very dangerously, observing Japanese naval movements and reporting them by radio. They had to change residence frequently, and there was always a chance that the natives would need much time finding the man. So, as soon as evening arrived, Kennedy and Ross set out in the two-man canoe to search for PT patrols. However, they paddled out too far and were caught in a rain squall and capsized. Between the storm and the treacherous current, the two sailors had to fight their way back to Cross (Nauru) Island. They were bounced against coral reefs and Ross was bruised most painfully.

After spending an anxious night, they saw eight natives land on the island. One of the natives stepped forward and gave a letter to Jack Kennedy. It read:

"Have just learned of your presence.... I strongly advise that you return here immediately in this canoe and by the time you arrive I will be in radio communication with authorities.... Will warn aviation of your crossing...."

Kennedy had the natives row him and Ross to the little island on which the other nine men waited, to unload the supplies and small stove that the Coastwatcher had sent. Then he was hidden under a load of ferns in the natives' larger canoe and transported to the New Zealander's secret post. By radio, he arranged a rendezvous with some PT boats and by midnight he was transferred to an American boat.

On August 8, he directed the PT boat to the rest of his crew and under cover of darkness, all of them were transferred to safety. It had been seven days of deprivation and ordeal in a region that was actually under enemy control. Despite hunger, fear, and sunburn over most of their bodies, their morale had remained high, and they were heroes in every sense of the word.

Later, Lt. John F. Kennedy was awarded the Purple Heart and the Navy and Marine Corps Medal. Admiral William F. "Bull" Halsey signed the commendation, which read, in part, "His courage, endurance, and excellent leadership contributed to the saving of several lives, and was in keeping with the highest traditions of the United States Naval Service." It would be difficult to estimate how many hours he spent in the water seeking to effect the rescue, or how much his determination and resourcefulness contributed to the morale of the survivors.

Yet he was always extremely modest about this episode in his life. In later years when someone asked him how to become a hero, he smiled and said, "Just have a boat sunk under you." When the fine movie *PT 109* was made about this feat, he was very careful to see that the script gave credit to all his men, and that this episode was treated as only an example of the bravery that so many Americans displayed in the South Pacific. He knew that there were outstanding instances of bravery performed by many Marines and sailors under actual battle conditions and under gunfire and he wanted no undue glory. Still, his willingness to suffer for his country in whatever way was necessary, marked him a patriot, a real American, in the finest sense of our tradition.

He was soon back on duty, but the rigors of his ordeal had weakened him and he fell ill with malaria. His weight went down to 125 pounds. But most serious of all, his back had been injured again in the accident, and he had to keep silent about it, or face the possibility of being relieved from duty. In December of that year, 1943, he was rotated back to the States and was assigned to the PT school near Miami. He had some leave coming, so he headed for the family estate at Palm Beach. It was a joyous reunion that Christmas, for Jack had been reported missing in action at about the very time that he was rescued.

Fortunately, at that time Joe Kennedy had not told Rose and the family, since there was a slight hope that he might be found. Jack had wired home that he was safe, but gave few details to the family, other than that he wanted to get more PT duty. During his last two months in the South Pacific, he was given command of PT 59, and four of his old crew volunteered to serve with him. They took part in several gun-boat maneuvers, and in barge-hunting. It was part of their job to support the Marine invaders and keep Japanese supplies from filtering through. The PT 59 was an old boat, constantly in need of repair, and that was actually Jack's biggest headache. The entries in the log in Kennedy's handwriting, kept making terse mention of repairs to the hull, the screw, or the gun, which was now part of the PT equipment.

So Christmas of 1943 brought some happiness to the Kennedy family. Joe, Jr., was in England, a navy pilot, and Bobby was an enlisted man in the Navy, but the rest of the family could look to the Christmas season for a few moments rest from the activity of war. They were proud of Jack, for he could have been home months earlier, but he had volunteered for extra time in the South Pacific, and only malaria finally sent him home. When he returned as instructor at the Florida PT base, his back began troubling him again, and he was prevailed upon to see the Navy doctors about it.

The Navy medics could not be fooled by Jack's determination to put up with the pain in his back. In the spring of 1944 they sent him to Chelsea Naval Hospital near Boston for a disc operation on his back. This is always a touchy operation with no real assurance of success. As it turned out, his back was to give him varying degrees of pain all the rest of his life, and he was almost always in need of some back support or brace. He would never again be able to indulge completely his love for sports, but his iron determination saw him through many trying days.

He spent many, many months on his back, recuperating to the point where he could spend some time at the family home in Hyannis Port. He was there on August 2, 1944, a year to the day of the ramming of his PT boat, when two priests arrived to talk to Joe, Sr. The three men went into the den, and when they came out just a few minutes later, all the family could read tragedy on the father's face. Joe, Jr., was now reported missing in action.

The father and mother clung desperately to the hope that this would be a second false report, as it had been in Jack's case. Actually, there never was any doubt, for Joe, Jr. had volunteered to fly what amounted to a suicide mission. The Navy had sent him to England in September of 1943, where he flew a Liberator bomber over the North Sea on submarine patrols. His patrols took him from the North Sea to the Bay of Biscayne. When his required number of missions was complete, he refused the offer of rotation home, and, as Jack had done, volunteered to stay on in his area of operations.

In July, 1944, he was ordered to return to the States, but he heard of a challenging attempt that was to be tried. The V-2 rockets were destroying London and their launching sites had to be exterminated. They were so heavily guarded that the manned bombers could not get through. It was decided to load a bomber with thousands of tons of TNT, head it for the launch area, and have the crew parachute into the English Channel where, it was hoped, they would be picked up.

It was a bold answer to an insurmountable danger, and no one would be commanded to attempt it. Joe Kennedy volunteered to pilot the plane, along with Lt. Wilford Wiley of Fort Worth. They managed to get the plane off the ground, but as they passed out into the Channel, above Dover, two tremendous explosions rocked the plane. After that, there was silence, and no bodies were ever found. There simply was no hope for their survival, and Joe, Sr. and Rose soon had to accept this as a fact.

1944 brought another great sorrow to them, as well. In June, Kathleen had entered into a civil marriage with the Marquess of Hartington, the oldest son of the Duke of Devonshire, one of the oldest Protestant families in England. Joe, Jr., had attended the wedding of his sister to William Cavendish, even though the rest of the family opposed it vigorously. A month after her husband was fighting in the front lines, and even while Kathleen was home comforting her parents, she received a cable informing her of his death. They had had only a month together and now she was a widow.

She returned to England and became, to all extents and purposes, more of a Cavendish than a Kennedy. Amidst all the grief of that tragic year, Rose Kennedy could feel that, somehow, her family was beginning to break up. In 1948, when Kathleen was flying to the Riviera to visit with her dad, the plane in which she was flying crashed into a mountain-side and she was killed instantly. The whole family was present in England when she was buried beside the husband whom she had had for only one month. In his future years, whenever John Kennedy was in Europe, he took time out to visit her grave in England.

But in 1944, Jack Kennedy had a personal battle to win. Since his back operation was only partially successful, he could resign himself to life as a semi-invalid, or he could look around to find a vocation in which his dreams and his determination, his ideals and his ambition, could be put to the greatest possible use. He rejected the first course of action in no time at all, but the second course demanded specific answers, and they were not easy in coming.

During his convalescence, Jack wrote a small book as a tribute to his older brother, called, As WE REMEMBER JOE. There seems to be no doubt that Jack had some suppressed feeling of guilt in his relationship with Joe. Joe was successful in everything he ever attempted. His studies were brilliant, his athletic record was first-rate, his personality, charm, and social ease were almost legendary. He was his father's favorite and the hope of the family name and fame.

Jack grew up in the shadow of this brilliance, and it took him many years to learn to trust himself and strike out on his own. Even then, in those first months and years after Joe's death, Jack used to say often, "If Joe were here, he'd do it this way..." or, "Joe would know how to handle this...." It was, indeed, a difficult stage in John Kennedy's maturing. Yet, he loved his older brother with a fierce, Irish pride. Even when they were competing against each other, Joe's triumphs were appreciated. And, should

JOHN F. KENNEDY, AMERICAN

any outsider ever criticize Joe, he would face Jack's complete wrath. But, the fact remains that Jack and Bob were much closer, always, despite the difference in their ages. They seemed to know and appreciate each other's strong points, and to complement each other's ideas. Jack and Bob were a team.

So, in the little book of remembrances, Jack poured out his inner feelings for Joe. All the things he would have said, if he could, came out in print in the precious little volume published by the family. Jack collected the reminiscences of many people who had known and admired Joe, Jr., and the sincerity of these tributes leaves no doubts about the tremendous potential that Joe had.

In death, Joe inspired his younger brother in a way that would have been impossible in life. After the grief of contemplating such great promise, caught up and cut short in the useless slaughter of war, the haunting idea kept returning—does this potential die with him—and, who will take it up? The conclusion was inescapable. Jack Kennedy must continue where his brother had left off. It would be Jack's own version of it, of course, tempered with an understanding of human beings that Joe in his brilliance might have missed, but the mantle was passed on and all the steely will of Jack's determination was now called forth.

It wasn't quite as simple as that, of course, for the grief of 1944 lingered on in the Kennedy family for many, many months. The Navy discharged Jack in 1945 because his back would never again permit him to undertake active Naval duty. He immediately took a job for International News Service as a correspondent. William Randolph Hearst, the owner, was a good friend of Mr. Kennedy's, so it hadn't been difficult to secure the position.

John Kennedy remained an INS reporter only for a few months, although they were exciting months. He covered the founding of the United Nations in San Francisco, where he foretold the weakness of that organization. He saw that East and West did not trust each other, and until they did, the UN would be restricted in its effectiveness. With his sense of history, he recognized the spirit of Versailles at the end of World War I, and even though he knew what a wonderful thing it would be for the world if the UN could be made to work, he saw the greed and selfishness that were working against it. He also mentioned talk that we would be fighting the Russians in ten or fifteen years. Fifteen years later, he would be fighting to preserve peace, and working to strengthen the United Nations.

In the summer of 1945, Jack traveled to Europe to cover the Potsdam Conference and the British election that removed Churchill from office in the middle of that important meeting. After that, Jack stopped in Dublin to file his last story, and then returned to Hyannis Port. Joe Kennedy had now pulled himself together, and he and Jack sat down to chart the future. It was, of course, a future in politics, and one that had only one goal. Success!

4

PUBLIC SERVICE

What is a politician? For some people, politics is a dirty word and the politician is a self-seeking man of small intellect, anxious to line his own pocket with the tax dollar. For a real American, politics is the chance to serve the people and make democracy work; it is a sacrifice of time, talent, and money to make the American dream a reality.

Actually, the United States throughout its history has had both extremes in its politicians, with every possible varying shade in between. There were the idealists of the late eighteenth century who wrote the Bill of Rights and the grasping clan that ruled in Reconstruction days, after the Civil War. Boston had seen both kinds of men, the honest patriot and the ward boss. In 1945, Boston was emerging from boss rule, but the names Kennedy and Fitzgerald were still magic in many parts of the city. So was the name Curley. And the Fitzgerald Democrats and the Curley Democrats were old enemies.

But sometimes, politics can offer strange twists to history. James Curley had been mayor of Boston for many years before he decided to run for Congress from the eleventh district, a solidly Democratic area in Boston. However, in Congress he was only one man among many, without any particular seniority, the life-blood of Congressional power. Curley decided to get his old job back as mayor of Boston, and, strangely enough, old Honey Fitz backed him. When the forces of these two men worked together, they were unbeatable, and, with Curley back in City Hall, the eleventh Congressional seat was vacant.

Thus was the way prepared for Jack's entrance into the political arena. When Curley heard the decision, he threw up his hands and said, "Tell him to get an apartment in Washington!" The Curley forces were indebted to the Fitzgerald and Kennedy forces and it looked as if Jack could just walk into the job. It wasn't that simple, at all, but with work, it could be made simple.

Jack threw himself into the work with the voice and vigor that were characteristic of him. First he had to establish residence in the district, and even then, he faced the charge of "carpet-bagger" that was later to plague his brother, Bob, in New York state. But the Kennedys were among the first families of Boston Democrats, even as twenty years later they were to be the real first family of every state in the nation.

Then he had to form his own organization, for he did not want to be the creature of any ward bosses. His friends gathered around him from Harvard, Choate, and his old PT squadron. They came from California and Maryland, from Republican and Protestant strongholds, to help Jack campaign in an overwhelmingly Catholic Democratic district in New England. And Jack had to learn to face crowds fearlessly and express himself decisively, and attend rallies unendingly. There were times when he longed to be back in the South Pacific, facing only a known enemy. There were times when he wished only that young Joe could have been there, doing the job for which he had been trained.

He had eight opponents in that first primary and every imaginable charge was levelled against him. The money that his father poured into the campaign brought sneers of "poor little rich boy."

His wartime record was brought up and examined, as well as his academic career. The whole family jumped into the fray, and Bobby and Teddy were immersed in practical politics for the first time. The Kennedy smile became a prime political asset, and after the first round of hand-shaking, Jack grew daily in self-confidence and assurance. His father and grandfather watched in delight and amazement.

In general, he ran on a moderately liberal Democratic platform, a position in which he was consistent all his life. He adopted few of his father's conservative positions, but he learned to temper youthful zeal by considering, seriously, positions opposite to his own. He left no stone unturned in order to meet his constituents, going to coffees, teas, and neighborhood parties. It paid off, for on primary night, Jack rolled up 22,000 votes to the 32,000 for his eight opponents. The eleventh congressional district of Massachusetts had elected a statesman, a man who was to bring honor to all of them.

But Kennedy's initial impact on Washington was very mild. There were jokes about his youth and his independence, and, definitely, about his casual, even sloppy dress. It was the story of Choate all over again, for Jack couldn't care less what he wore, or what he looked like. He was as much at home in khaki fatigues or a business suit, and he was apt to wear either to the floor of the house.

His sister Eunice moved into the rented Georgetown house to act as his hostess, and she stayed with him until she married the now-famous R. Sargent Shriver. Margaret Ambrose was the housekeeper, and the faithful George Thomas was his long-suffering valet. His closest friend on the Hill was another freshman Congressman, George Smathers of Florida. While he enjoyed the social life of Washington fully, he seldom went out with the same girl twice, and his keen, quick mind never seemed to tire of official business.

He set up an efficient staff in his Washington office, and another in Boston. His people knew that they could count on Kennedy, and this young man who was only twenty-nine when he was sworn into office, was returned to office in 1948 without a single opponent, and in 1950 by a majority of five-to-one. True, he built up a terrible record of absenteeism during his career in the Congress, but he never tired of airing his views, or of electioneering. He was always running for some office, even if he wasn't sure what it might be. He had decided almost as soon as he went to Washington that he would not be a Representative for long. Whatever the future might hold, he was determined to be ready for it. He seldom, if ever, turned down a speaking engagement or a tour, or a chance to meet people.

His relations with the dean of the Massachusetts delegation started off cool and became colder. Representative McCormack, a bosom pal of President Truman, was more apt to get word of his young colleague from the headlines in the Boston papers than from the CONGRESSIONAL RECORD. Kennedy owed his good committee assignment on the Education and Labor Committee to McCormack, but Jack did not feel that he therefore had to vote the McCormack line. Another committee member happened to be another freshman Congressman, Richard Nixon, and the two of them became reasonably familiar with each other's mode of operation.

No one could accuse John Kennedy of following any particular "line" in his work in the House of Representatives. Some questioned his sincerity, but no one ever doubted his independence. Some called him ambitious, but no one ever called him lazy or short-sighted. When he made politics his career and success his goal, he worked at it. As early as 1948 he started making himself known in the state of Massachusetts. Tony Coluccio, an old Harvard football team-mate, visited every city and town in the state, and Ken O'Donnell and Larry O'Brien, two of JFK's most loyal aides, set up Kennedy committees all across the state.

His legislative record in those three terms in the House was interesting. As a returned veteran, he fought for adequate housing measures against such varied interests as the real estate lobbies.

When President Truman, an old Army man, wanted to suppress the Marine Corps in the interest of economy, Jack leaped into the leadership fight to save the Corps. He would never forget the bravery of the average Marine enlisted man as he had witnessed it in the war. If the country ever needed men again to storm a Tarawa or a Guadalcanal, or to raise the flag on some other Iwo Jima, JFK wanted the Marines around, spirited, cocky and prepared.

He fought legislation that would hurt labor, yet voted for bills that would reform labor. He voted for economy measures and backed the Marshall Plan to provide aid to foreign nations that were faced with economic ruin and Communist treachery in the post-war world. He fought for school lunch programs, but voted against Federal aid to education when it did not offer equal help to parochial schools. He knew that education is a responsibility of the parent, and aid from public funds should help parents educate their children according to their own conscience, not force them all into public schools.

But Jack was setting a torrid pace for himself, and by 1950 it was beginning to tell on his health. There were days when his back was so bad that he had to hobble around on crutches. He was spending Monday to Thursday each week in Washington, and the long weekends racing across his home state. In O'Brien and O'Donnell he had two of the most knowledgeable men on the American scene for political managers, and, in Massachusetts, Coluccio and Furcolo (later to be governor) to guide his steps. He never let them down in their plans for him, or their faith in him, and sometimes he would hobble to a stage door in great pain, only to lay down the crutches and stride on stage with his great grin, as if he were ready for a swim or a fight.

In 1952, the next great challenge came, and the four years of intense campaigning were to pay off. Strangely enough, at the beginning of that year, JFK couldn't have told you what office he would be running for. In the spring of that year, Governor Dever decided to run for re-election instead of challenging the incumbent Republican Senator, Henry Cabot Lodge. Dever felt that Lodge was unbeatable and so he didn't want to risk his political career. This left the way open for Kennedy, and he announced his candidacy.

Henry Cabot Lodge was a formidable foe. What the Kennedys and the Fitzgeralds were to Boston politics, the Cabots and the Lodges were to Massachusetts Republicanism. In 1936, when FDR won with the largest landslide in history, Lodge beat Curley for the Senate seat by almost one hundred-fifty thousand votes. Lodge's grandfather had been Senator from Massachusetts for many terms, and he had led the fight to keep America out of the League of Nations, an action which probably hastened President Wilson's death, and which certainly caused the downfall of the League, and helped lead to World War II. But the younger Lodge's name was famous, his friends many, his career distinguished, and his war record excellent.

This was the man that Kennedy faced. His years of preparation were put to the test, and his organization stood up to it. Lodge had been an early Eisenhower supporter and when Ike was nominated to run for president in 1952, Lodge became his campaign manager. He did not spend much time in Massachusetts fighting the young Catholic from Boston who, he thought, was little known outside the big city. Lodge was a proven vote-getter and popular with his people.

But suddenly, disturbing reports started coming in from the precincts. In haste, Lodge rushed back to Massachusetts, but it was too late. In every town, he found that Kennedy was known and had spoken. Indeed, all the Kennedys were at work, Bobby, Teddy, and the girls. Rose hosted receptions, and Joe Kennedy called in old friends who owed him favors. The Taft Republicans, bitter at Lodge's desertion of their conservative candidate, gave their support to the personable young Kennedy.

It was a bitter campaign, and an expensive one. The Kennedys spent over seventy-five thousand dollars of their own money and raised almost half a million more. The Republicans spent over a million dollars, and even brought Eisenhower to Boston for a gigantic rally on the night before the election. But the voters knew Jack Kennedy. Eisenhower swept Massachusetts, and the nation, and every Republican on the state ticket was elected, except Lodge. Even Governor Dever, who had sought a safe position, was defeated. But John Fitzgerald Kennedy won his Senate race by over seventy thousand votes and became a power in the Democratic party of Massachusetts.

However, the power and glory of his victory seemed to fall into second place because of an event that had happened about seven months before. He had met Jacqueline Lee Bouvier at the home of mutual friends, Charles and Martha Bartlett. It was not a case of love at first sight, nor was it even an especially successful first meeting. Yet, her haunting beauty, her quiet grace, her charm and her smile kept coming back to the young Congressman. During the hectic days of his senatorial campaign, he took time to find out more about her. Everything he discovered interested him more and more, and he began to find excuses to meet her a little more often.

Jacqueline was in Washington as a reporter for the WASHINGTON TIMES-HERALD, their "Inquiring Camera Girl." She captivated the people she interviewed and she was always welcomed back by them for more news. She scooped the press with her intimate interviews of the Eisenhowers and the Nixons, and she was popular with other reporters as well. It is legendary in Washington that she wanted to interview Ted Williams in the locker room after a game with the Washington Senators. The male sports reporters finally talked her out of it.

The girl who is "Jackie" to the whole nation, if not the whole world, came from the Social Register set and had the highest connections in society. When she made her debut in 1947, the famous columnist Cholly Knickerbocker called her "#1 Deb of the Year." She has one sister, Caroline Lee Bouvier, now the Princess Radziwell. Her parents were divorced when she was only ten, and her mother married John Auchinloss, which brought Jackie and Lee into the large family groupings at Merrywood, her step-father's luxurious estate in the horse country of Virginia.

She had a lifetime interest in horses, and, indeed, in all animals. Her love of the arts and music is well-known. She had attended all the "right" schools and the right events during her years of growing up. But when she was nineteen, she rebelled at the stifling confines of the social whirl and struck out on her own. Finally this brought her to Washington to her job as a reporter. She had been offered a position with VOGUE, the fashion magazine, in Paris, but she refused it. She said that her love of Paris was so great that she just might decide to stay there for life.

Humanly speaking, Jacqueline and Jack should have met many years earlier, for their families had mutual friends in great numbers and they were both accepted in society. Both of them were talented, athletic, cultured and wealthy. Yet their paths never crossed, for Jackie enjoyed art, music, and horsemanship, while Jack moved in more active circles, especially politics and aquatic sports.

Senator Kennedy returned to Washington with thoughts of Miss Bouvier as his first order of business. Few people knew how often the Senate's most eligible bachelor and the popular lady-reporter saw each other, or how often they slipped out of Washington for dinner and dancing. They both enjoyed the theatre and she revived Jack's interest in concerts and symphonies. Then it was her turn to leave Washington, for her newspaper sent her to London to cover the coronation of Queen Elizabeth II. During this enforced separation, John Kennedy made up his mind, and when Jackie stepped off the plane that brought her back to this country, he proposed to her. And she accepted at once.

From that moment on, there was no privacy. The mad whirl of parties and publicity began, and, while Jack was used to this, it was a terrible trial for Jackie. Her love for people is genuine and sincere, and her devotion to worthwhile causes amounts to real dedication, but her temperament is such that she needs sufficient privacy to be able to sort out the thoughts of her own heart. This very quality of inner peace and assurance is one of her most attractive characteristics, and one that brings people flocking around her.

And they certainly did during the summer of 1953 after the wedding date had been announced to the press. She was already something of a "darling" for the Washington press corps, and Jack Kennedy was young, virile and popular. It was a romance made to order for the newspapers, from the columnists to the society editors. LIFE magazine sent reporters and photographers to cover the couple, and the July 20, 1953 edition carried a front page picture of them. In later years, the Kennedys were to appear often on the cover of LIFE, but this was Jackie's introduction to life with the Kennedy clan.

The wedding itself took place on September 12, 1953 and their vows were witnessed by Richard Cardinal Cushing at St. Mary's Church in Newport. Almost 5,000 people gathered for the wedding, with 800 of the invited guests attending the reception afterwards. VOGUE devoted a whole page just to Jackie's beautiful face, and the society reporters let themselves go in describing her ivory silk tafetta gown, the tiara of orange blossoms and lace, and her grandmother's veil. Her sister Lee was the matron of honor, but there were a dozen bridesmaids and two dozen ushers. It was definitely the social event of the season.

They flew to Acapulco for their honeymoon, a lovely Mexican town that was just being discovered by American tourists. It was a beautiful beginning for a marriage that was to be a ten-year love affair.

Not that it didn't have some difficulties and a few crises, but Jackie, in looking back at their first year, admitted that the period of adjustment was "hectic but fun." Being married to a Kennedy meant travel, people, meetings, parties, politics and athletics. It meant belonging to the American people and becoming involved in anything and everything that faced the nation.

That first fast pace was really too much for both of them. Jack's old back ailment was getting much worse and Jackie's casual and relaxed attitude was being deluged with activity. They really had no home of their own until later, when, for a few years, they settled happily in Georgetown. But at first, Cape Cod, Virginia, the Riviera, even California and Georgia, could claim large parts of their time. With only a few moments notice, Jackie might find herself with a hundred guests, or whisked off to Miami to a convention. Because of her seeming self-sufficiency, Jackie did not attract close intimate friends, but Jean Kennedy, who was by then Mrs. Smith, became and remains one of Jackie's closest confidantes. It helped to have someone to unburden herself to. But life itself finally taught the young Kennedys a much-needed lesson.

It was a series of calamities that slowed down the hectic, happy life. Jackie's distaste for the active family athletics of the Kennedy homestead was climaxed and her participation stopped after she broke an ankle at touch football. Then, a year after the marriage, Jackie had a miscarriage. And finally, the Senator's back became so bad that he was forced to go back to the hospital. The doctors feared that a spinal fusion might kill him, but that he would become more and more crippled if there were no operation. Finally, Jack himself decided that he would take the risk.

In the fall of 1954 the first operation was done in New York by a team of experts. The long convalescence began, interrupted only by a trip, on a stretcher, to Palm Beach to spend Christmas with the family. Shortly after the New Year, the second operation was performed, and, while it did not fully correct the situation, and he would always have to depend on a brace or even, from time to time, crutches, the danger of really being a cripple was overcome. During all this time, Jackie was his eyes, ears, legs, and constant companion.

During this long recuperation, Jack wrote the book PROFILES IN COURAGE, for which he was to receive a Pulitzer Prize. Actually, he considered the work a team effort. Another faithful and brilliant aide who had been added to his staff was Ted Sorenson, and Ted haunted the Library of Congress doing the basic research. Jackie acted as literary editor of the manuscript and she proved to be a severe critic, demanding that only the best writing would do.

The book was a series of biographical sketches of famous Americans who stood up for the principles of justice and fair play, even at the risk of their political futures. JFK himself had to face that decision seven years later when he entered into the struggle for a Civil Rights Bill. But meanwhile, he was writing about great American patriots such as John Q. Adams, Daniel Webster and Robert Taft. The book was published by Harper's the following year, and it became a best seller immediately. It has been translated into dozens of foreign languages to introduce the spirit of American patriotism to peoples all over the world. The prize money that he won for the book was given to the United Negro College Fund.

It was during these six months that Jack and Jackie molded themselves into the flawless team that they became. The love that they had exchanged before God's altar now matured into that deeper and stronger love that defies definition. Even while he was sick in bed, Jack needed activity, and the book and some of his basic senatorial duties kept up his spirits. But the long hours that the young couple spent with each other, reading aloud, discussing ideas, or just listening to each other's dreams and goals, these hours were a precious blessing in which they united their hearts and souls in an eternal union.

In the spring of 1955, Jack returned to the Senate floor, to be welcomed back, enthusiastically, by Vice President Nixon, Senate Majority Leader, Lyndon B. Johnson, and Senator William Knowland. The Senate recognized his courage and rose as a man to applaud him.

But almost immediately Jack was involved in a fight for his political life. His upset victory in 1952 had marked him as a top leader in the Democratic organization in Massachusetts, but the most powerful voice in the state organization was that of the House Majority Leader, Representative John McCormack. Jack's real base of power was still centered in Boston itself. The McCormack family had ambitions just as strong as the Kennedy or Curley groups. But the Curley faction was now past history, and old "Honey Fitz" was more of a legend than a power. McCormack decided to take active control before the Kennedy organization became too powerful.

What he didn't realize was that the Kennedy organization was already too powerful for him. McCormack put in his own man as chairman of the state party and began to organize against Adlai Stevenson's bid for renomination in the coming 1956 national convention. Jack Kennedy, Bob Kennedy, and their loyal aides went to work. It was a bitter intra-party battle between a strong and entrenched McCormack, and the youthful zeal and innate political ability of the Kennedys. When the votes were counted, the Democratic politicians voted overwhelmingly for the Kennedy forces. McCormack didn't give up easily, and a few years later Ted Kennedy had to battle a McCormack for his Senate seat. However, long before JFK was assassinated, he and John McCormack had become friends, and the

House Majority leader gave loyal support and firm leadership to the Kennedy legislative program in Congress.

Meanwhile, Eisenhower's first term was coming to a close, and the national political scene was becoming more active. 1956 was going to be a difficult year for the Democrats. They seemed to have all the issues, but Eisenhower had the popularity.

Jack Kennedy was plummeted into the middle of the national scene that year, and he entered it with real enthusiasm. As he and Jackie, again pregnant, left for Chicago and the convention in August, they actually were beginning their march to the White House.

5

THE CAMPAIGN TRAIL

The Kennedys arrived in Chicago in mid-August 1956 to take part in the excitement of the Democratic convention. The party faithful always see an election year as one that favors their side, but the country was under the spell of Ike, and the professionals knew that it would be a hard, desperate, uphill struggle to unseat him. While there were grumblings about the type of campaign that Adlai

Stevenson had conducted in 1952, the great majority of the Democrats in Chicago were devoted to him and wanted to see him try again.

Stevenson, in his own way, is as remarkable a phenomenon in American politics as are the Kennedys. He is one of the most intellectual men to seek the presidency in the twentieth century. His devotion to his principles keeps him from making many of the compromises that practical politicians demand of him, and his devotion to the United States and the United Nations makes him a statesman of world renown. For wit and humor, and for a real grasp on the actual world in which we live, he has almost no equals on the national or international scene.

But while the young intellectuals might be "madly for Adlai," the country as a whole stood in awe of his intellect. The people simply couldn't identify themselves with this man, and he was destined to be defeated in 1956 by an even greater margin than in 1952, even though the Democratic Party itself carried many more congressional and state candidates than in 1952. John Kennedy was a loyal Stevenson man, the leader of a powerful state delegation, and already starting to make a national reputation for himself. Stevenson and Kennedy were intellectual equals with many common, progressive ideals.

Adlai was nominated on the first ballot and the maneuvering for the vice-presidential spot began.

Jack and his friends swept into action. Jackie, who was feeling miserable, stayed with her sister-in-law, Eunice Shriver, and for several days she only saw her husband on television. Jack had narrated the campaign film that opened the convention and then, without previously being notified, a Stevenson aide called and said that Adlai wanted Kennedy to nominate him.

Jack and Ted Sorenson worked all night on the speech, and with only a few hours of sleep, Jack went to deliver it. The delegates liked the talk, and were pleased that this rising young Democrat was given such an honor. Most thought it would end there, for that year, and many thought it was enough acknowledgment of the Kennedy loyalty to Adlai. But the Kennedy group was never one to miss an opportunity.

Adlai could hardly reach over the heads of many of his senior followers to take JFK for the second spot on the ticket. So, the Kennedy followers went to work on Stevenson to open the convention for vice-presidential nominees. This appealed to him in principle, and it allowed him to hold himself above any factions in the party. The Kennedy forces had won a real victory which they were quick to follow up.

The Kennedy family went to work. Most of them were in Chicago, but Joe, in France, got on the phone and called his friends. Peter Lawford, the husband of Pat Kennedy, called his friends, long distance, from California, where he and Pat were awaiting the birth of a baby. The Kennedy aides and allies were holding strategy meetings and swinging into high gear.

Two Senators from Tennessee were the front runners, Kefauver and Gore. The Mayor of New York, Robert Wagner, and Hubert H. Humphrey a Senator from Minnesota, were the other two rivals. All four of them were professional politicians, well-known and well-liked. Many Southerners, however, feared that Estes Kefauver was too liberal, so, the Kennedy team went to work on the South. In order to stop Kefauver, many of them joined the Kennedy forces, and Jack went into the convention floor with significant strength.

Humphrey had started his national career as an ultra-liberal, and while he had matured and abandoned the extreme position, it was to take eight more years for him to live down his youthful excesses. Wagner was considered a big-city "boss" and he was never able to gather into his fold many delegates from outside New York. Senator Gore was the candidate of the conservative Democrats, so the moderates and the stop-Kefauver forces gathered around Kennedy.

On the first ballot, Kefauver led Kennedy by over 175 votes, with Gore, Wagner and Humphrey quickly falling into relative ineffectualness. On the second ballot, Kennedy went ahead of Kefauver, just 68 votes short of the nomination. Kentucky switched to him and he was 38 votes away. But no one else jumped on the bandwagon, so the third ballot was called. The Kennedy party was jubilant, but Kennedy himself sensed that he had just reached his peak.

On the third ballot, Gore decided that loyalty to his fellow Tennesseean was important to his own political future in the state. He switched to Estes Kefauver. In the Missouri delegation, there was anti-Kennedy sentiment because he had frequently criticized their native son, President Truman. Missouri switched from Humphrey to Kefauver. With that, the vice-presidential nomination went to Estes, and Jack was on his way to the convention podium to move that it be made unanimous.

It had certainly been a trying time for Jack and Jackie. Mrs. Kennedy felt too ill to travel, so she went to Newport to stay with her mother. Jack was exhausted from the fight and needed a rest, so he flew to the Riviera to board a yacht. This was the first time he had ever lost a political battle and it hurt, deeply. The chance had come so quickly that the Kennedy organization, usually fast and efficient, had been caught off guard. Jack and Bobby were never again to make that mistake, and their plans were started already for the 1960 convention.

Yet this was a fortunate defeat. Kefauver was known across the country because of his TV crime investigations. Had Adlai declined to run, Estes would have been a probable choice. But even with his popularity, the Eisenhower victory was greater than before. Had Jack been the second man on the team, his youth and his religion would certainly have been blamed, and he would never have been President. Ike was simply unbeatable in 1956, and Jack was saved from what would have been political disaster, if not national oblivion. But at the same time, of course, this was unknown, and Jack rushed off to nurse his wounds.

And then there was another personal disaster. Jackie had another miscarriage, and this time, her own life was in danger. Jack hurried back to the States and began the vigil at her bedside, as she had done at his. Twice Jackie had been at his side when he was anointed, with death staring him in the face. Now he knelt and prayed for her, and their future.

Their married life was to be an even closer union than before. They each consciously tried to adopt the other partner's interests. When Jackie recovered, she went to Georgetown University to take courses in political science. Jack began to take seriously to the art, music, and reading that Jackie liked. Jackie took lessons in water sports, especially boating and water skiing. Jack began dressing more carefully. In so many ways, big and little, they continued to deepen their love, and they discovered that they were extending and strengthening their own personalities, as well.

By Thanksgiving of the next year, little Caroline was born, and both parents thanked God for the safe deliverance. She was the answer to their prayers and the proud father could hardly be contained. In the Georgetown home, a new Kennedy family was begun. Jackie's previous trouble made this child more precious than ever.

1958 was another election year, and Jack was up for re-election to the Senate. This time, Jackie traveled with him, and she soon proved that she was a tremendous political asset. By nature, Jackie would not have cared for this activity, but once she made up her mind, she surpassed everyone's expectations at her adept way of handling crowds. In fact, she rather surprised herself, for she actually found herself enjoying it. She also began to fall in love with Massachusetts and to share Jack's love for the American history that seemed to live on there. And Bob Kennedy used this campaign to test out many of the ideas he would use in 1960, and again for himself in New York state in 1964.

That campaign was crowned with great success. Jack won by almost 900,000 votes, the largest plurality ever given to a candidate in Massachusetts. A landslide victory such as this could not escape national attention, and the Kennedy organization publicized it for all it was worth. With Jackie now fully convinced of the importance of life in politics, Jack could devote himself to the coming effort.

The Democratic Party was faced with some difficult choices as it moved toward the presidential year. In a sense, there was a leadership vacuum.

Stevenson's supporters were loyal to the bitter end, but the vast majority of Democrats did not want to unite behind him for a third try. The irrepressible Hubert Humphrey was interested, as was the stately and dignified Senator Stuart Symington of Missouri. A belated entrant was Lyndon Baines Johnson who had the powerful professionals behind him. As usual, Mayor Wagner was mentioned, and several lesser figures, whose campaigns never left the ground.

While President Eisenhower could not succeed himself, his image alone would be difficult to beat, and Vice-President Nixon was, himself, an attractive candidate for the Republicans. He would be difficult to defeat, for it was obvious that he would make a good president. Therefore, the Democrats had to find a man who could unite all elements of the Democratic Party, which was notorious for its factional fighting.

This was the situation into which the Kennedy organization injected itself. No one single man emerged as head and shoulders above the others, and Jack Kennedy had several grave obstacles to overcome. The most obstinate was that he defied a label. Even his most fervent followers could not, in conscious, call him a devoted liberal or a dedicated conservative. He was, simply, a typical American, independently moderate and progressive in the great mainstream of American history. He was that fascinating contradiction of a man who is an idealist, but practical; a realist, but a dreamer.

The liberals blamed him for not joining in the censure of Senator Joe McCarthy, a man who had started the work of awakening the people of the United States to the dangers of Communist infiltration. McCarthy performed a valuable service to the country when he started his work, but he developed into the type of fanatic who saw a Communist behind every tree in Washington. His work, unfortunately, quickly sank into extremism, and he was responsible for a reign of terror that revolted most people of good will and decency.

The Senate of the United States finally had to censure him, officially, for his excesses. John F. Kennedy was in the hospital for one of his back operations at the time, but the liberals felt that he should have put it off until after the vote. Kennedy, himself, later was to say that had he guessed how important this vote would become, he would have had himself carried into the Senate on a stretcher to vote against McCarthyism.

Both liberals and conservatives were confused by Jack's attitude toward civil rights. His devotion to the underdog was never questioned, but some questioned the means he would use to implement his interest. On key points of the 1957 Civil Rights Bill he had frequently voted with the South, including a provision for jury trials that the liberals thought softened the bill. It never seemed to occur to them that his devotion to America's heritage of trial by jury and his sense of history made this a natural for him.

Jack Kennedy had to court support in the South. His religion, alone, could alienate that sector of the country, and, in a rough election, the South could hold the key to victory. No honest politician can ignore this area in the nation any more than he can ignore his own principles. Kennedy was not the only one who has been placed in this dilemma. Nor must one forget the conservative position of Joe Kennedy. Jack was once asked by a reporter if he agreed with his father on many issues. Jack's answer was "Practically none," but the fact remains that in such a close family, the attitude would be there and would have to be considered. All told, the liberals found Kennedy too conservative and the conservatives found him too liberal.

The question of religion was to haunt the Kennedy organization throughout the campaign. Back at the 1956 convention the Kennedys had prepared a brief on the so-called Catholic vote, and had circulated it. It is to their everlasting credit that Catholics in America do not vote as Catholics; they vote as Americans. But this can be difficult to prove to those who dislike or distrust the Church.

According to the statement issued in 1956, Catholics tend to vote in larger percentages than other religious groups, but they vote for the candidate of their choice, not in blocks. The way these Catholics vote tends to have great importance be-

90

cause they live in great numbers in large cities and key states. As for the defeat of Al Smith, which was often used as proof that a Catholic could not win, the 1928 campaign included the issue of Prohibition and was conducted in a year when there was peace and prosperity, against Herbert Hoover, a gentleman of great experience and distinction. It was simply not a case of voting for or against a Catholic, as such.

The campaign of bigotry and prejudice that anti-Catholic groups might conduct will cause as many people to vote against bigotry as might vote for it. Thus, they cancel each other. John Kennedy had such faith in the American people that he felt they would rise above extremism and vote for the man they felt best qualified, despite his religion. The 1956 statement was circulated widely among professional politicians in the years following, and it finally had the impact that its compilers intended.

During 1959 and 1960, Kennedy criss-crossed the country in his San Diego built Convair airplane, talking to groups in every section of the country. Jackie went with him and again proved herself a regular campaigner. At times, when Jack had to be in the Senate for a vote, she appeared in his place with great success. Then, as the convention drew near, Jackie became pregnant again, and with her past history of trouble, Jack insisted that she remain at home under constant care.

To win the nomination, Jack had to prove to the party leaders that he was a vote-getter outside of his home state, and that the religious issue could be overcome. This meant that he had to take the "primary route" and enter state primaries in various places. He won easily, and by the time the convention opened he had close to 700 delegates' votes committed to him.

At Los Angeles the Kennedy organization left nothing to chance. Bobby and Ted had the memory and experience of 1956 when their organization fell apart under stress. This time they had every key man and every delegation covered by one of their aides, and they had their own communications system. Now it was their opponents who had to face the pressure and come up with a way to stop Kennedy from taking over on the first ballot.

The Stevenson supporters turned out in great numbers, for southern California was one of their strongholds. Adlai broke precedent and appeared among them. They chanted and shouted and tried to stampede the delegates. Mrs. Roosevelt used her considerable influence for him, too, but while he was a sentimental favorite, it never went beyond that. Former President Truman backed Stuart Symington with all his power, but Symington simply did not have popular appeal. He might have made an excellent compromise candidate had there been a stalemate, but since these various forces did not unite behind one single candidate, they helped defeat the anti-Kennedy forces.

Lyndon Johnson was the late-comer in announcing his candidacy who almost did the trick. Beyond a doubt his experience, his record, and his connections made him an excellent choice for the position. The only thing against him was his civil rights record as a Southerner. This was so serious that it proved to be the obstacle he could not surmount. However, in gathering all his strength for the fight and in garnering the anti-Kennedy movement's votes, he almost succeeded in his bid for the nomination. If he could have convinced the liberals that his moderate conservatism could include a real civil rights stand on the national level (as it actually did when he became President in 1963) he would have won.

The Pennsylvania delegation, large, powerful and uncommitted, invited Johnson and Kennedy to appear at its final caucus before the balloting began. Lyndon told them of his career, his voting record, his support of the Roosevelt and Truman programs, and his experience as Majority Leader. He pointed out Kennedy's youth, relative lack of experience, and frequent absence from the Senate. It was a powerful speech, and many of us who saw it thought that he had certainly won Pennsylvania. But Jack strode to the rostrum, grinned his best Kennedy smile, and simply congratulated Johnson on his marvelous record and urged that he be left in the Senate to continue the fine work he was doing. It was masterful, and Pennsylvania joined the Kennedy fan club.

Millions of TV viewers sat on the edge of their chairs as the convention began to vote. The outcome was far from certain, and it was all too possible that the 1956 scene would be repeated; that he would come within a few votes of winning and never be able to go over the top. Some of the delegations were committed to him by law for the first ballot, but were known to be luke-warm. If he did not win on the first ballot, he might never win at all. Even as the voting started, Bob Kennedy was hurrying around from one delegation to another, gathering a vote here, keeping a vote there, answering doubts and reassuring the worried.

The work certainly paid off, for half-way through the counting, it was obvious that enough secret strength had developed to put Jack over the top. The hard work of Bob Kennedy and his Lieutenants, and the personal charm of the candidate had captured the convention. By the time Wyoming voted, Jack was "in" and he finished with 806 votes, to 409 for Johnson and about 300 divided among the others. Even as Wyoming was casting its votes, Jack was on the phone calling Jackie at Cape Cod. A few minutes later she went out to talk to the press, as Jack left his rooms to go to the convention.

The next order of business was the choice of a vice-presidential nominee. The logical choice was between Symington and a fine young Senator from the state of Washington, Henry M. Jackson. Both had strength and a good following and both would have been fine running-mates. Stevenson was out, although, again, his followers would have been pleased. But Kennedy wanted the best man, one who would make a fine president if necessary, and one who would help him get elected. That man was unquestionably Lyndon Johnson.—Would he accept? He had said that he would never leave his powerful Senate job for the somewhat ceremonial position of vice president.

Early the next morning Jack went to Lyndon's room and woke him up. He said, quite simply, "I need you." Johnson replied, "Do you really want me?" "Yes." And it was settled. Johnson threw himself into the campaign with complete dedication and there is no doubt that he carried the South, appeased the conservatives, calmed the liberals and made victory possible. Kennedy never had a more loyal follower. Johnson came to have a high regard for the younger man, a real friendship, and a commitment to the Kennedy program. Probably that speech to the Pennsylvania delegation had convinced JFK that Johnson was presidential timbre, but it was a fortunate day for the country when Kennedy made the decision to join forces with the great Texan.

Vice President Nixon was chosen by the GOP. A Westerner, he turned to the East for a running mate to balance his ticket. He also chose a fine man who would be a capable candidate, even a capable president, if necessary. He picked Henry Cabot Lodge, whom Kennedy had upset in 1952, a cultured, liberal, and experienced man. But the battle was joined, a battle of giants, of great Americans, of youth. It was one of the most exciting campaigns in the history of the country, and one of the most expensive.

The Kennedy camp was used to action, but now it was intensified. Bob Kennedy seemed to be everywhere and to know everything. Ted Kennedy, who had had a real baptism by fire in the 1958 campaign, became an expert in handling the details of a campaign. The Kennedy girls, sisters and sisters-in-law, went on speaking tours. Rose poured at teas and talked at coffees. Sorenson wrote speeches until he began to dream of typewriter ribbons, and still he wrote on. O'Brien and O'Donnell formed the "Irish Mafia" and the team seemed tireless.

Only Jackie was restricted. Her appearances were few and far between because of the precious son she carried, for John-John was to be born in a few short months. Jack tried to keep everything calm and quiet around her, and while he was seldom home, he called her constantly. No one came from the Hyannis Port headquarters without first telling news of Jackie. When the press wanted to play her up as the typical wife and mother, she refused. She was an individual who loved her husband and home, but she didn't like to cook, she didn't like to do housework, and she was grateful that she had a nurse to help with the family work—Caroline alone, then.

The campaign trip was a blur of movement for both major candidates. Dick Nixon had made the mistake of promising to go to all 50 states. Kennedy concentrated on the areas where the largest number of voters lived and where his strength was good. The enthusiasm he generated there worked like magic. Television came into its own, too, and both men used it to good advantage. Nixon was a seasoned campaigner and a tough opponent. He neither gave nor asked for mercy!

The television debates between the two men definitely favored Kennedy. It gave him an opportunity to be seen by countless millions. They were both good debaters and the results were probably even, but the publicity helped Jack more than Dick. Eisenhower was brought into the campaign too late to sweep the nation. Nixon was hospitalized for about ten days at the height of the campaign. The Kennedy party capitalized on each of these things and, in an election as close as this turned out to be, who can say which item was most helpful? The pollsters and the political prophets were helpless in the face of such activity. No one could guess the outcome.

The religious issue was much more bitter than either party could have believed possible. It is to the great credit of both parties that they did not exploit the issue. It is difficult to believe how many millions of pieces of bitter bigotry poured from the presses. Nixon was embarrassed by it and Kennedy tried to counteract it politely. He appeared before a ministerial meeting in Houston to give his views on Church-State relations, and they were typical of what any American Catholic would hold. The Church must stay out of politics and the politicians must stay out of ecclesiastical affairs. And the Church itself certainly maintained an absolute neutrality. But, of course, you can't convince fanatics by reason, and many strange charges were made. As St. Peter wrote to the early Christians, the only answer that ever convinces is good example, and the Kennedys proved themselves fine Americans and fine Catholics.

Nixon started the campaign with all the obvious advantages, but the Kennedy wit and charm brought people to listen, and his ability to handle complex issues with skill and clarity won them over. Both men poured their hearts into the race, and by the time November rolled around, they were each living on about four hours of sleep a night, and hastily gulped hamburgers. How either man lived through that campaign is hard to explain! In these days of modern communication, there is no longer the need for a long campaign. Issues can be brought to the attention of millions on radio and TV. Even two and a half months seems unnecessarily long in modern times.

On election day, the madness was over. Jack and Jackie voted early at a booth located in the West End branch of the Boston Public Library. Then they returned to Hyannis Port, posed for a few pictures, and retired behind a wall of silence. Jack walked next door to Bob Kennedy's house where a communications center had been established. He played touch football for a while with Bob and Ted, walked the beach, played with Caroline, talked with his father. It was a new and different tension he felt that day, different from the past months of rush and crush. Bob Kennedy and Lou Harris, the famous pollster, started analyzing the results from key centers across the nation as soon as they started to come in. The first results were depressing.

Slightly under 70,000,000 people voted in 1960, the largest free vote the world has ever known. It was better than 10% above the 1956 total. But the early afternoon reports showed Nixon slightly ahead in the fast opinion sampling that was being done. Jack and Jackie ate a leisurely dinner together for the first time in many, many months. They were joined by Ted Sorenson and, from time to time, other close friends and associates. At 11:30 Jackie went to bed, cheered by what she saw on television, but worried by the depressed look on the faces of the party's leaders. The polls were still open in the far West, and counting was just beginning in the Mid-West. Jack went back to Bobbie's house.

Dick and Pat Nixon had also voted early that morning in their Whittier, Calif., precinct. They, too, knew the let down of pressure. Dick slipped away from the crowd with close friends and drove to San Diego, and then across the border to Tijuana, Mexico for dinner. For a while that afternoon, the press couldn't even find him, but after posing for pictures with Tijuana's mayor, he began a relaxed drive back up the coast, enjoying the 120 miles of beautiful Pacific Coast shoreline, through La Jolla and Del Mar, through the great Marine Corps base at Camp Pendleton, San Clemente, San Juan Capistrano and the great freeways into Los Angeles.

When he returned, the polls in the East were long since closed, and the reporters were reading off the huge popular vote that Kennedy was receiving. But his campaign managers did not look worried at all. These were big city votes, typically Democratic, regularly the first to report, and not representative of the key precincts around the country that the professionals watched. On both coasts, the party headquarters were filled with top men with worried brows.

As midnight passed in Massachusetts, Kennedy was assured of 241 electoral votes out of the 269 he needed for election. But with every report, Huntly and Brinkly on NBC could only report narrow leads see-sawing between the two men in the states which held the balance of power. The 30 telephones in the Robert Kennedy house could give no more definite leads. At about 3:00 A.M. Jack had 261 sure electoral votes, with Michigan, Illinois, California, and Minnesota unpredictable.

But it was midnight in Los Angeles, and it was obvious that the final close states would remain unknown factors until the last precincts were in. It was that close a race. Dick and Pat Nixon appeared on television. Those who stayed up and watched all night as the returns came in wondered if a concession was in order, but Nixon refused to concede. Pat Nixon brushed a tear from her eyes, and the candidates on both sides of the nation went to bed. Kennedy refused to claim victory, too.

Bob Kennedy, however, was one of those who did stay up all night, telephoning his contacts everywhere. By dawn, Michigan was in the Kennedy column, and the battle was won. The next day it looked as if JFK had even won California, but the counting of absentee ballots finally gave it to Nixon, a week later. By 7:00 A.M. the Secret Service men had surrounded the Hyannis Port cottage, and Kennedy was the 35th President of the United States.

The election was close. Kennedy won by one-tenth of one percent of the votes with a popular lead of slightly over 100,000 votes. Nixon actually carried more states, but they had fewer electoral ballots. In some key states Kennedy's margin was so slight that re-count movements were started, and some of the die-hard papers that had supported Nixon, as in

Southern California, refused to give the term "President-elect" to Kennedy until the electoral college vote was certified.

But in the Kennedy family it was a time for rejoicing, and within the month a new son had been added to the family. There was no end to the happiness as Jack and Jackie looked forward to the greatest challenge that can come to great Americans.

6

"MR. PRESIDENT"

The President's term in office may not begin until January, but his work begins the moment it is certain that he is elected. The day after the election, of course, was a day for simple acknowledgement and realization of the tremendous honor. But by the next day, suddenly, the change has been wrought. Even Bobby leaped to his feet when Jack entered the room for this first formal meeting with his aides—the Presidential aides. From now on he is addressed by even his closest friends as "Mr. President."

The first order of business was to plan for the orderly transition of business from one administration to another, from one party to another. Kennedy had looked forward to this possibility and shortly after his nomination he had phoned Clark Clifford to begin making such a blueprint of action for him. Jack never liked to face crises unprepared, and one of his great strengths was that even in the middle of one battle, he was looking forward to the next. He had done that in 1956, for instance, when he went to the convention with a brief on the Catholic vote, just in case it might be needed.

Clark Clifford was a close friend of Stuart Symington's and he had been Truman's White House Counsel. He had also been Kennedy's lawyer when Drew Pearson had suggested on television that PROFILES IN COURAGE had not been written by Kennedy. Clifford had quietly and efficiently forced an immediate and complete retraction from Pearson. Clifford's 50-page brief was the pattern for continuity in government as 1960 turned into 1961.

The next order of business was the appointment of a Cabinet to form the highest policy-making level in the Federal government, as well as over one hundred second and third level positions. Often the men on these levels are the key men in putting the plans of the President and the Cabinet into effect. Kennedy was determined to have the greatest talent in the nation put at the service of the nation and he did not hesitate to cross party lines to do this. He held conferences on the matter of appointments with his top advisors, taking them with him from Massachusetts to Washington to New York and to Palm Beach, Florida.

The joyful interruption when John, Jr. was born was not allowed to interfere with his duty to the nation. Like every proud father, when asked the name of his first son, he almost stuttered, "Why, John Fitzgerald Kennedy, Jr., of course. She already decided—ah, it has been decided, John, of course." But much as the whole nation took this family to its heart, he was their President, and his work was endless.

On November 18th, he was told of the plans to invade Cuba. He was never at ease, or satisfied with this idea, but it seems that Mr. Eisenhower was so sure that Nixon would win and would continue his policies, that he did not hesitate to plan so drastic an action during the turn-over of a presidential tenure. It was most unfortunate, as subsequent events were to prove.

The "inner" groups that worked with John Kennedy during these two months before the inauguration were the men upon whom he had depended for the past few years. Clark Clifford was the only newcomer to this most influential group. The others were the familiar Bob Kennedy, Sargent Shriver, Larry O'Brien, Ralph Dungan, the likeable Pierre Salinger, and, of course, Sorenson and O'Donnell.

Luther Hodges, a Southern businessman became Secretary of Commerce, and Stewart L. Udall of Arizona became Secretary of the Interior. Robert S. McNamara, president of the Ford Motor Co., was appointed Secretary of Defense precisely because of his administrative ability. The Pentagon spends over half the national budget, and JFK wanted it spent wisely and economically. The appointment of an Attorney-General caused the most agony.

There was no doubt in the President's mind that Robert Kennedy was the finest man for the job. He had worked for his brother all his life, as his counsel when he was on the Crime Investigations committee, as his campaign manager and his master strategist. They were inseparable. But the criticism of favoritism is hard to live down, and Bob finally decided to turn down the appointment. This was one of the few times in years that Joe Kennedy stepped in and urged something on the boys. He told them that they did need each other now more than ever. Robert Kennedy still hesitated, and he consulted J. Edgar Hoover at the FBI, Supreme Court Justice William Douglas, and others. He still wanted to refuse, to spare Jack any embarrassment, but the President wouldn't take no for an answer. The Kennedy wit put the critics off, for JFK admitted that his brother "should have some experience before he has to go off and practice law." It was an excellent appointment.

The Secretary of State is one of the most important positions in government, and Dean Rusk was brought from the presidency of the Rockefeller Foundation to take this office. He was a world-oriented man who was not afraid to speak up. The hard-working Orville Freeman came from Minnesota to head the Agriculture Department. Republican Douglas Dillon went to the Treasury, David Bell to the Budget Bureau, and the knowledgeable John Kenneth Galbraith to India, as Ambassador. Ribicoff came from Connecticut to head the Health, Education and Welfare Dept., and so on. The finest talent that America could uncover was assembled for the New Frontier, the name JFK had chosen for his goals for the country.

Whatever criticism there was of the new Cabinet and Administration centered on the fact that they tended to be too conservative, and lacking in glamor. No one can deny, however, that they were the most intelligent and industrious a group ever brought together to run the government. The Kennedys themselves supplied the glamor and the new ideas, and these were undeniably brilliant.

The inauguration day approached quickly and the tempo of anticipation grew with it. The orderly turnover of government was underway and the program for the day itself was mapped out. Five gala inaugural balls were planned, a magnificent parade, hosts of dignitaries to be feted, and world situations to be watched. Both the home in Georgetown and the White House were scenes of activity. Kennedy took off for the home of an old family friend, the artist William Walton, one of the men who had helped him wait out election night. There was an inaugural address to be written, one that would tell the nation and the world what sort of man the new chief executive was.

January 20, 1961 was a bitterly cold and snowy day. Jack started the day with Mass at Holy Trinity Church, then went to the White House for coffee with Dwight and Mamie Eisenhower. Finally there was the ride to the Capitol, the solemn swearing in ceremony conducted by Supreme Court Justice Warren. Richard Cardinal Cushing had prayed a mighty prayer for guidance, and Robert Frost, the great New England poet had set the tone of hope and greatness. President Kennedy then approached the microphones to give his first address to the nation. In it were evident his two great loves, his God and his country.

He said, in part, "The same revolutionary beliefs for which our forbears fought are still at issue around the globe—the belief that the rights of man come not from the generosity of the state but from the hand of God. We dare not forget today that we are the heirs of that first revolution. . . . The torch has been passed to a new generation of Americans."

He committed himself to the defense of human rights everywhere, at home, in Latin America, and in the new nations of the world. He assured our friends and allies that we would stand true and firm, and he warned our enemies that he would be strong and courageous. He pledged to the United Nations that America would help make it a great instrument for peace in an atomic world.

"Let us begin anew," he said, when it comes to solving the problems of the Cold War, never fearing to negotiate, but never negotiating from fear. He recognized that the problems seemed insurmountable, and he knew that in the first one hundred days of his administration it would not be ended, this senseless competition, nor in the first one thousand days, but "let us begin."

At home he called for a war on the "common enemies of man: tyranny, poverty, disease, and war itself." He summoned all men of good will to help him in these great tasks. "The energy, the faith and the devotion which we bring to this endeavor will light out country and all who serve it—and the glow from that fire can truly light the world.

"And so my fellow Americans: Ask not what your country will do for you—ask what you can do for your country.

"My fellow citizens of the world: Ask not what America will do for you, but what together we can do for the freedom of man." And he concluded with a prayer and an appeal. "Let us go forth to lead the land we love, asking His blessing and His help, but knowing that here on earth God's work must truly be our own."

In fourteen minutes it was over. There was no campaign oratory about it, only outright sincerity. No one was left unmoved by it, and all felt the surge of promise that this young man held for the future of his native land. He was dedicated to prayer and good works, to confidence in God and in the talents that God had given him. His heart was filled with a burning love for America, a love so great that he wanted to share America's greatness with the whole world.

The rest of that day saw the end of his private life and the beginning of his public life. No one could have guessed that these "first one thousand days" were to mark all the rest of his time on earth, and that he would never again have any really private life. Jackie returned to the White House to begin her life as First Lady and to begin to take her place in the hearts of her countrymen. As she roamed through the mansion that day, she began to form the plans that would turn it into a real American shrine.

Jack had to attend the endless inaugural parade, smiling and waving. Then there were the five balls to attend, and more people to share the joy of the great day and wish him well. He stopped to see an old friend, Joseph Alsop, on his way home, and that night, the President of the United States walked into the White House to begin the work toward which his whole life had pointed.

That work began the next day, with an early top security meeting on the crisis in Southeast Asia. Then it was Laos, later it would be Cambodia, and finally South Viet-Nam. President Truman came to call, and so did Mayor Daley of Chicago. The White House staff began to feel its way into the routine of the new administration, and the "old timers" gasped in dismay at the whirlwind that was JFK. If he wanted someone, he went after him personally. If a photographer missed a picture, the President allowed re-takes. One night he slipped away to go to his brother Robert's home for a quiet dinner. The Secret Service and the press corps never knew what to expect next.

But soon the New Frontier began to settle down to its own rules. The newness was over and the novelty gone. Daily the work grew heavier, and JFK seemed to have an inexhaustible supply of energy. He read everything, starting with ten newspapers a day. Memos and work papers and task-force papers, whatever their length, were read and analyzed by JFK himself. He did not wait for someone else to make digests for him. A fourteen-hour day of work was not at all unusual. He was always easily accessible to the press, and the television press interview became a regular procedure. He looked forward to them, and so did the reporters and the nation. One of the reporters, Mae Craig, became nationally known because of her exchanges with the President and the quick flashes of wit that she brought forth from him.

The "honeymoon" period for JFK (the designation that he himself suggested to the press) and the New Frontier was over quickly. As Congress reassembled, many of the bitter incidents of the campaign remained in some legislative minds. The great Sam Rayburn, Majority Leader of the House, backed Kennedy completely, but the narrow margin of victory and the President's youth made it difficult for many Congressmen to cooperate. The nation fell more and more in love with the First Family, but Congress didn't.

When it became apparent that the Republicans and conservative Democrats were going to bottle up the Kennedy legislative programs, Jack and Bobby declared a private war. Joe Kennedy had once said, "Jack works as hard as a human can, and Bobby works a little harder than Jack." When the two of them went to work on the House Rules Committee, it was a battle to the blood.

In the Congress, men receive committee chairmanships not on the basis of ability, but simply through seniority. Conservative Democrats, mainly from the South, are re-elected year after year, and even though they usually vote with the Republicans, they become senior "Democrats," and hold most of the committee chairs. The House Rules Commitee is one of the most powerful, since it determines which bills will go out to the floor of Congress, and when. An arch-conservative headed this body, and for him, any hint of "liberal" legislation smacked of treason. Add to this the fact that he was no Kennedy fan, and it can be seen how easily JFK could be thwarted.

The Kennedy brothers used every trick that they knew, and all the powers of office, plus all the votes of their allies, and forced a vote through the House that enlarged the Rules Committee and added some liberal votes. This was a calculated risk, since Congress is jealous of its privileges and its liberties, and some key men might be alienated. However, this is an abuse of the Congressional power, and the New Frontier decided to face the issue immediately. This was one of the most courageous decisions that JFK had to make in his first days in the White House. Had he lost it, none of his program would have been turned into law. When he won it, he at least gained the advantage of getting some of his programs considered.

It is difficult for us to realize how much bitter opposition Kennedy suffered during his entire Presidency. While the nation, in general, backed him whole-heartedly, the entrenched interests of some politicians feared him. Some of his enemies started fighting the 1964 election immediately, and, history will show that some were more determined to embarrass him than to promote the national good. The problems at home and abroad were urgent, but the President needed the support of Congress to present the image of strength to the world and confidence to the nation.

In the first crucial test of his strength, the Kennedy victory came on the House Rules vote with only five votes to spare. The tally was 217 to 212. Sixty-four Democrats were against the President. Twenty-two Republicans crossed over and were for him. It meant trouble, trouble that lasted right through to his death. After he was gone, many of his programs passed quickly, and again, it is difficult to believe that there wasn't some degree of shame and guilt among his enemies for the way they treated him.

Problems of all sorts surrounded the President in those first days. In the Congo the Communists were trying for a massive take over and only the hand of the United Nations with the firm backing of the United States prevented this. But ultra-conservatives in the United States were so opposed to the United Nations that they actually made it easier for the Communists.

The Russians watched this new American leader carefully. Two captured American airmen were returned as a gesture of friendship, but JFK and Dean Rusk were aware that this might only be a cover for other activity. Communist activity in Cuba and in Latin America, generally, was watched carefully by the new administration. The space program was in difficulty, the domestic economy was lagging, and the image of America abroad was at a low ebb.

Kennedy's concept of help for Latin America was logical and realistic. He felt that foreign aid was necessary for the defense of the free world, and vital for the growth of freedom around the world. But he did not see foreign aid as a simple hand out. While it is true that eighty percent of the money spent on aid is kept in this country, spent on materials that are then sent abroad, nevertheless, the whole program is meant to help these countries stand on their own feet.

New nations, especially in Africa, may need outright gifts, just to get their economy started on a sound basis. Latin America, on the other hand, is a land of great contrasts—immense wealth in the hands of the few, terrible poverty for the majority. This is a natural breeding ground for Communism. Unless these unjust practices are ended, unless social justice grows, there is no hope for peace, stability and freedom south of the border.

The Alliance for Progress was the JFK answer. It is a long-range ten year program in which billions of dollars of American money will be sent to Latin America if, and only if, it helps these people help themselves. The governments must provide some of the funds and the land for housing projects to wipe out slums, for schools to combat illiteracy, for hospitals to combat disease. Programs like these actually help the people, not the wealthy few. The work and the money bolster up the local economy and begin a pattern of growth.

The Alliance is a revolutionary concept of magnificent proportions. Its long range possibilities are unlimited. But obviously it is not going to be popular with the rich ruling class. They will not benefit directly, and, indeed, they may even have to sacrifice some of their privileges as the lower classes begin the long climb to decent standards of living. Yet, they couldn't turn it down, either, for the people might revolt if there was outright rejection, and without American involvement, the Communists could take over in some countries in a matter of weeks.

The small minds of Kennedy's critics could not conceive the scope and magnitude of this program. The fact that there would be no immediate response from the use of all this money gave them a means of criticizing the President, and they did, openly and loudly. Nevertheless, this is the only way that Latin America can share in the economic prosperity of the United States and take its place in the free world as equal partners. Many of the bishops in South America recognized the tremendous value of this Alliance and began to lead the way in land reform. Pope John XXIII saw the need of cooperation and he asked that every religious order in the United States make plans to send ten percent of its personnel to Latin America in the next ten years, particularly to start schools. If the people and the Church in South America are saved, it will be because God raised up two world leaders, an American President and a Pope, who had world-wide vision and unlimited hope.

The space program raised the eyes of the nation even beyond the confines of the planet. When JFK took office, he found that the scientific know-how of the country was far beyond any other nation's, but the use of the information was lagging far behind.

Kennedy turned his mind to the problem, however, and saw space as the next frontier of the human mind and heart. He saw challenge and unlimited opportunity. He was intrigued by the unknown and fascinated by the possibilities of what might be discovered. On the diplomatic level he hoped that the planet Earth might have to compose its differences and approach the universe as a united race. On the military side, he recognized that the sole control of the upper atmosphere by one planet would mean an almost insurmountable advantage. On the political level, he saw that the Communist world could make great propaganda use of their space exploits, and impress the less sophisticated countries.

When Yuri Gagarin, a Russian, became the first man in space Kennedy decided to make use of the occasion and throw the United States into the race. It was a multi-billion dollar program, but the benefits for America were incalculable. Many timid souls were afraid of the program. Some scientists felt that they should be allowed to continue on a slow but steady pace, and allow the press to publicize their achievements in the fields of pure research. But for Kennedy there was no fear and no turning aside. America would never be a second class power, in any field, as far as he was concerned.

The pressure groups never let up in opposing his far-sighted and far-reaching programs. Such opposition only made him more determined to work for the good of his fellow Americans. Wherever his countrymen were sick, impoverished, or out of work, he was concerned, and he demanded that his staff and the whole administration turn its concern to the problem.

During those first few months, family life was begun in the White House for the four Kennedys. Caroline became the darling of the nation, and certainly the darling of the press corps. Her pets and her little parties, her remarks and her friends were always being quoted. She and her father were often pictured at play, and one of the most touching pictures shows her and the President at church on Sunday, coming from Mass.

John, Jr., grew up in the glare of the photographer's flash bulb. His baptism and his mother's theories on child care were equally newsworthy. It seemed as if the nation could not get enough news of this fine family. LIFE magazine ran a picture story on young John and his dad at "work" together in the president's office. For the most part, Jackie tried to keep as much privacy for the family as possible.

She wanted to be a worthy First Lady, and there is no doubt that she made an impact on the nation during her husband's term. The White House became, under her direction, a real national shrine, and she and a very select committee restored historical rooms and areas in the White House. Her influence on the cultural life of the nation will never be forgotten. Several times she traveled abroad, and she proved herself as adept at diplomacy as she had years before proved herself in politics. She swept Paris before her and held the crowds enthralled. When the President returned, he introduced himself at a breakfast as "The man who accompanied Mrs. Kennedy to France." She had triumphs in South America, and in Vienna, when the President met with Khrushchev shortly after his election.

The President has to entertain frequently, and often there must be formal dinners and receptions. But Jackie tried to emphasize the naturalness of a hospitality that she would have shown no matter where her home was. Her graciousness and her charm were unassumed; she never tried to be anything other than herself. If she invited someone for dinner, whether she was a young reporter or the First Lady, she would offer a cocktail and provide cigarettes. The society editors in Washington all praised her for this, because the custom had been that the White House parties were stiff and formal. A guest had to know the right people to get a drink, or step outside to smoke. Jackie would have none of this.

Pierre Salinger, the press secretary and personal family friend, found that he had to report Kennedy family news as often and as regularly as affairs of state. One Sunday night when the President invited all the lesser members of the administration to come to the White House to meet the family, and to bring along their own families, the press reported that at least eight precedents were set in that one evening. That didn't bother the Kennedys. The President told them all, "I want to meet the people I read about in the paper."

Informality was the key to White House procedures. Cabinet meetings and Security Council meetings were seldom called because JFK felt that each man was expert in his own field and aware of what was going on, but why bother him with the problems of other departments. When a battle was on, the Kennedy's were implacable. When they won, they forgave quickly and helped the "enemy" save face. Neither Jack nor Bobby nursed a grudge. When they lost, they accepted the blame and went on to the next event.

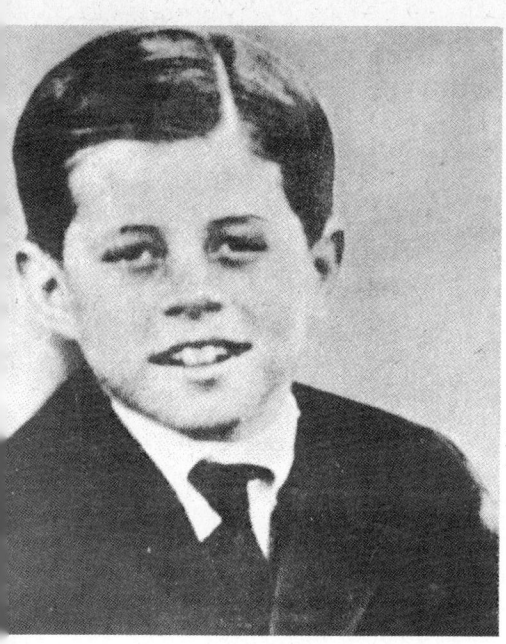

Nine-year-old John Fitzgerald Kennedy, born May 29, 1917, the second of the nine children of Rose and Joseph P. Kennedy.

John F. Kennedy and big brother, Joseph P. Kennedy, Jr. (left), almost two years his senior. The two were often rivals and Joe usually won their fights. John Kennedy learned much from his older brother, especially about handling people.

A Kennedy family portrait taken in 1938: **seated** (left to right): Eunice, Jean, Edward, Joseph P. Kennedy, Sr., Patricia, Kathleen; **standing:** Rosemary, Robert, John, Mrs. Rose Kennedy and Joseph, Jr.

The three most promising Kennedy children in London in 1938, Joe (left), Kathleen and John. Joe Jr. died flying an explosive filled bomber in World War II. Kathleen who was widowed in the war, died in an air crash in 1948. John was slain by an assassin's bullet in 1963.

Joe Junior and John Kennedy in the Navy in 1942.

Lieutenant Kennedy, nick-named "Shafty," in command of PT 109.

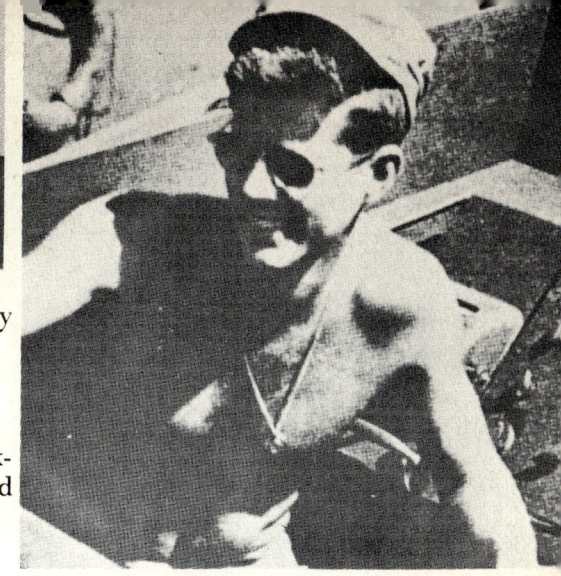

When his craft was rammed nd cut in two by an enemy de-troyer on the night of August ;, 1943, he risked his life to save nembers of his crew and was .warded the Navy Marine Corps nedal for gallantry in action.

A much-determined young man ready to fight his way
to the top—John F. Kennedy in 1946, after he announced
his candidacy for the Democratic nomination to Congress
from Boston's eleventh district. He was elected in 1947 and
re-elected in 1950.

In 1952 John F. Kennedy was elected Junior Senator from Massachusetts. Here he confers with an old family friend, the then Archbishop Cushing, during Harvard Commencement exercises.

Jacqueline Bouvier and John F. Kennedy in Hyannis-port on the day they announced their engagement in June, 1953. She was twenty-three and he was thirty-six.

Mr. and Mrs. John F. Kennedy leaving church in Newport, after their marriage by Archbishop Cushing, September 12, 1953.

The Newlyweds cutting their wedding cake, while brother Bob enjoys the scene.

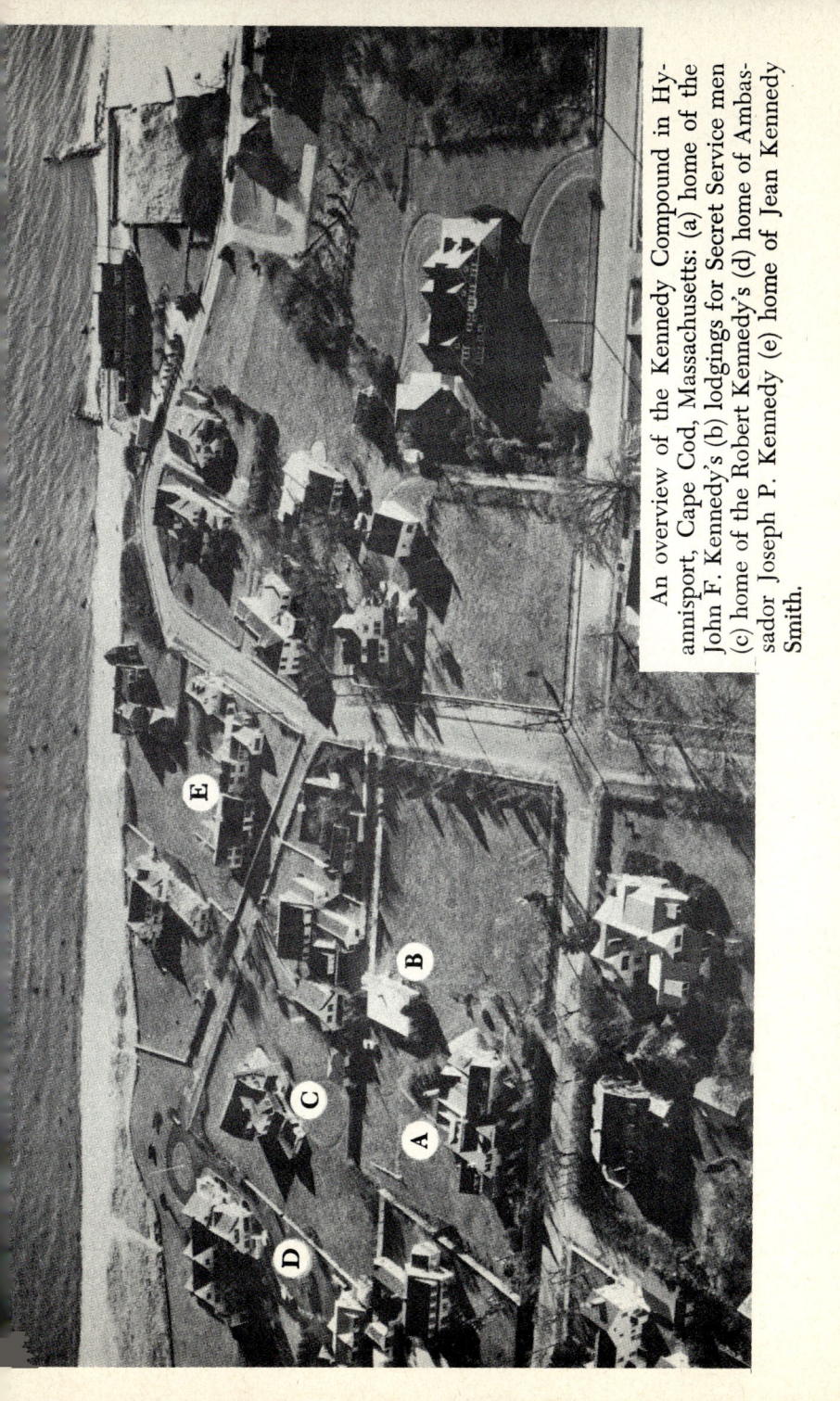

An overview of the Kennedy Compound in Hyannisport, Cape Cod, Massachusetts: (a) home of the John F. Kennedy's (b) lodgings for Secret Service men (c) home of the Robert Kennedy's (d) home of Ambassador Joseph P. Kennedy (e) home of Jean Kennedy Smith.

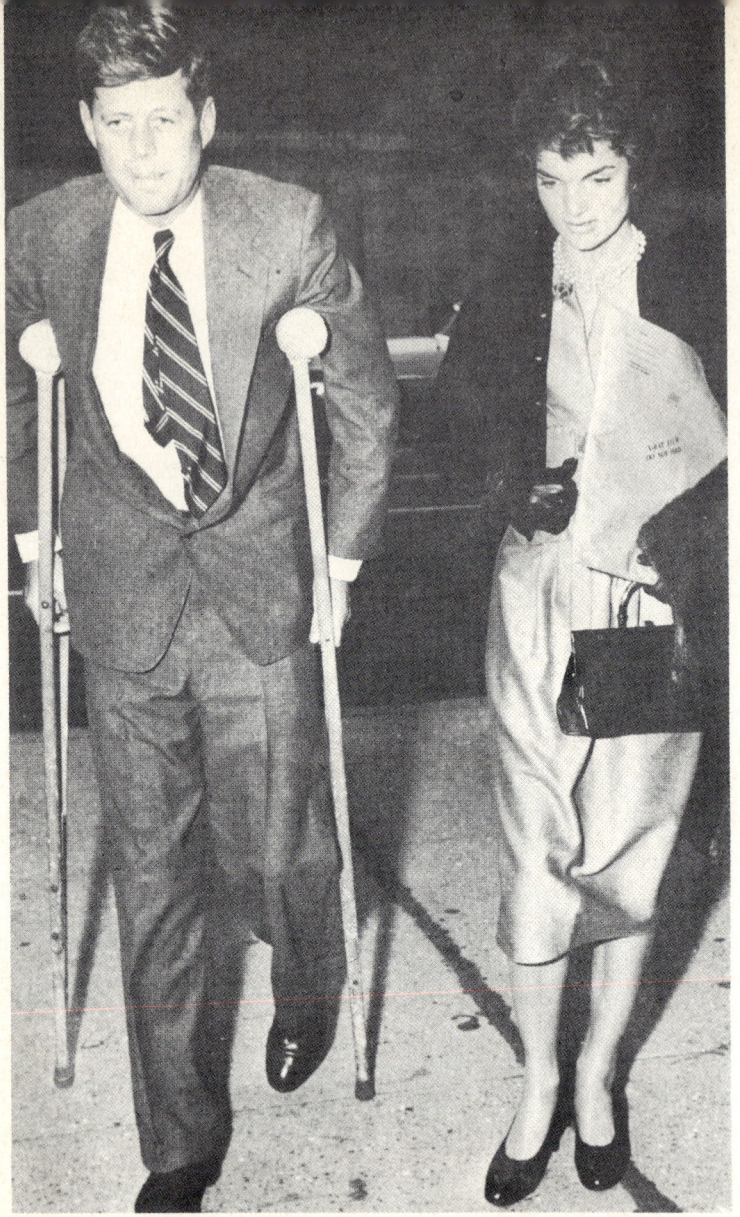

The recurrence of an old spinal injury paralyzed the young Massachusetts Senator from the waist down. Hobbling on crutches he went to a New York hospital for the first of two serious operations. Chances of his recovery were one out of ten. At the time of the second operation John F. Kennedy hovered close to death and received the Last Sacraments. During a long and painful convalescence he wrote the prize winning **Profiles in Courage.**

Jack and Jackie in Washington: a quiet Sunday in Georgetown; breakfast together before driving him to the Senate. When the long struggle began that led to the White House, they worked and fought side by side. In a rare photo of John F. Kennedy wearing glasses, he is dictating letters to Jackie who often helped out as a secretary.

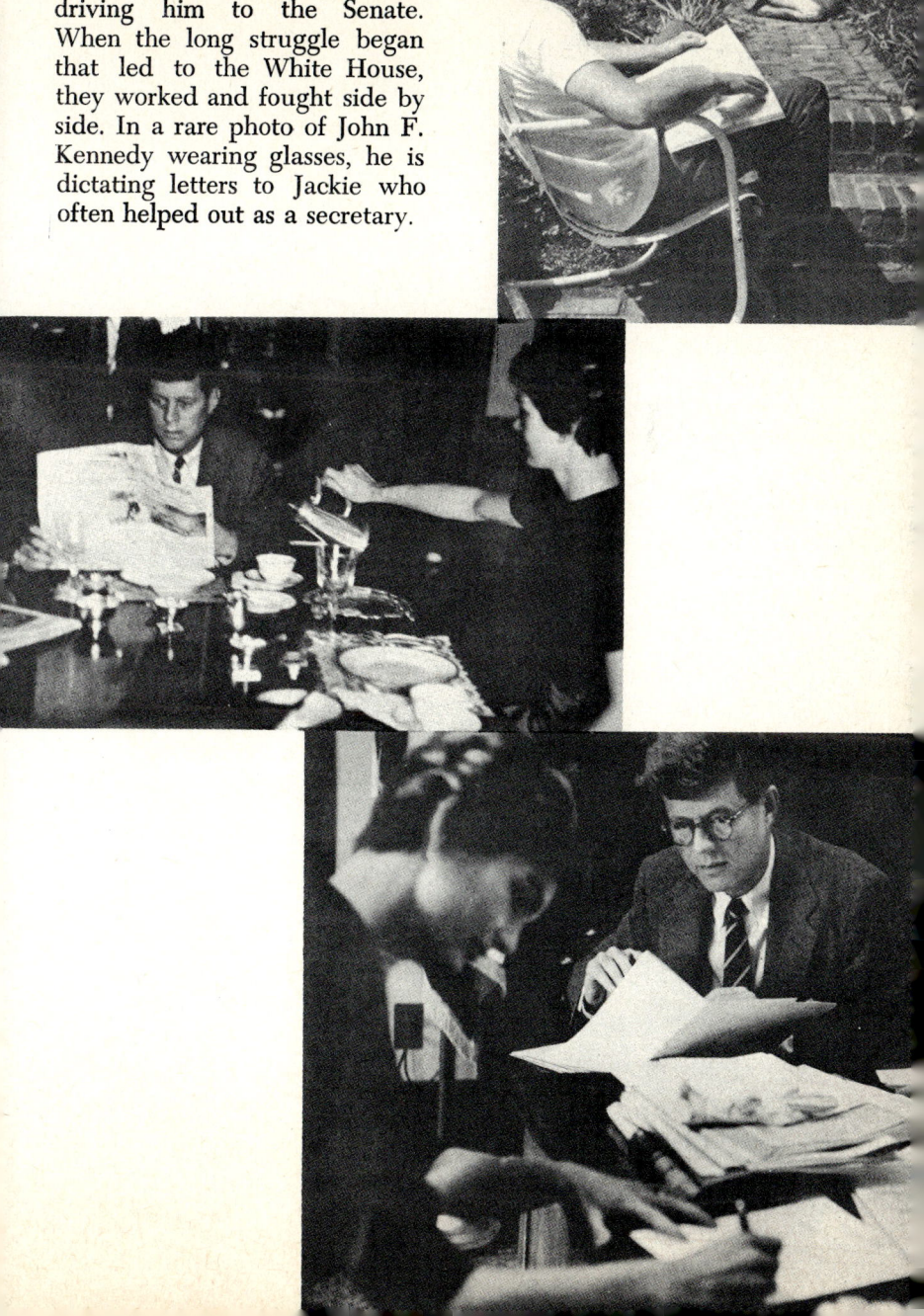

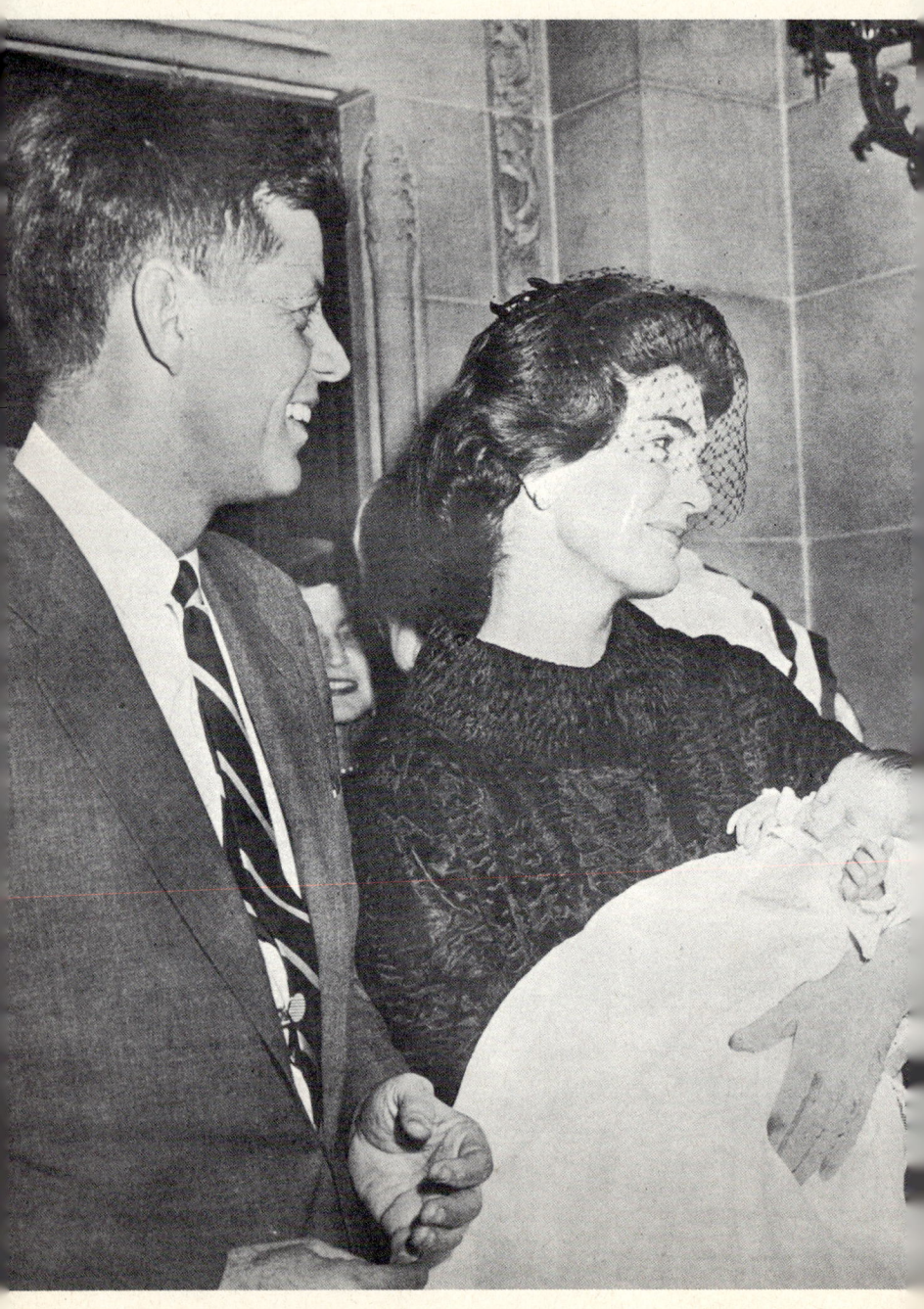

Archbishop Cushing and a beaming Jack and Jackie after the Baptism of their daughter Caroline, December 13, 1957.

No matter how busy his political schedule, John Kennedy always found a way to spend precious moments with his loving family.

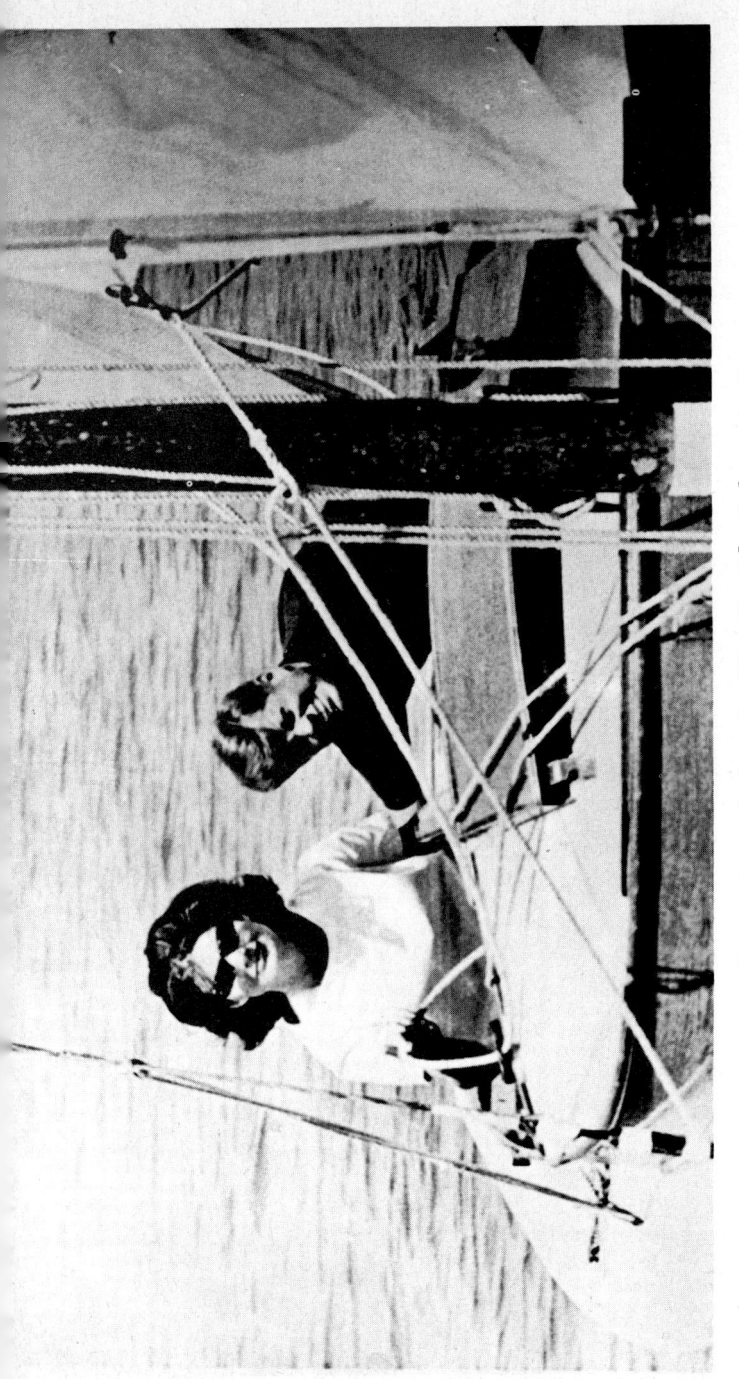

John F. Kennedy lost the *Vice Presidential* nomination in 1956 but four years later scored a major political triumph by winning the Democratic nomination for President. Here Jack and Jackie enjoy themselves on the sea he loved so well, during a short vacation before the long presidential campaign.

The 1960 campaign was one of the most outstanding in American history. John F. Kennedy covered thousands of campaign miles and with the help of the well organized Kennedy campaign machinery, became the thirty-fifth President of the United States.

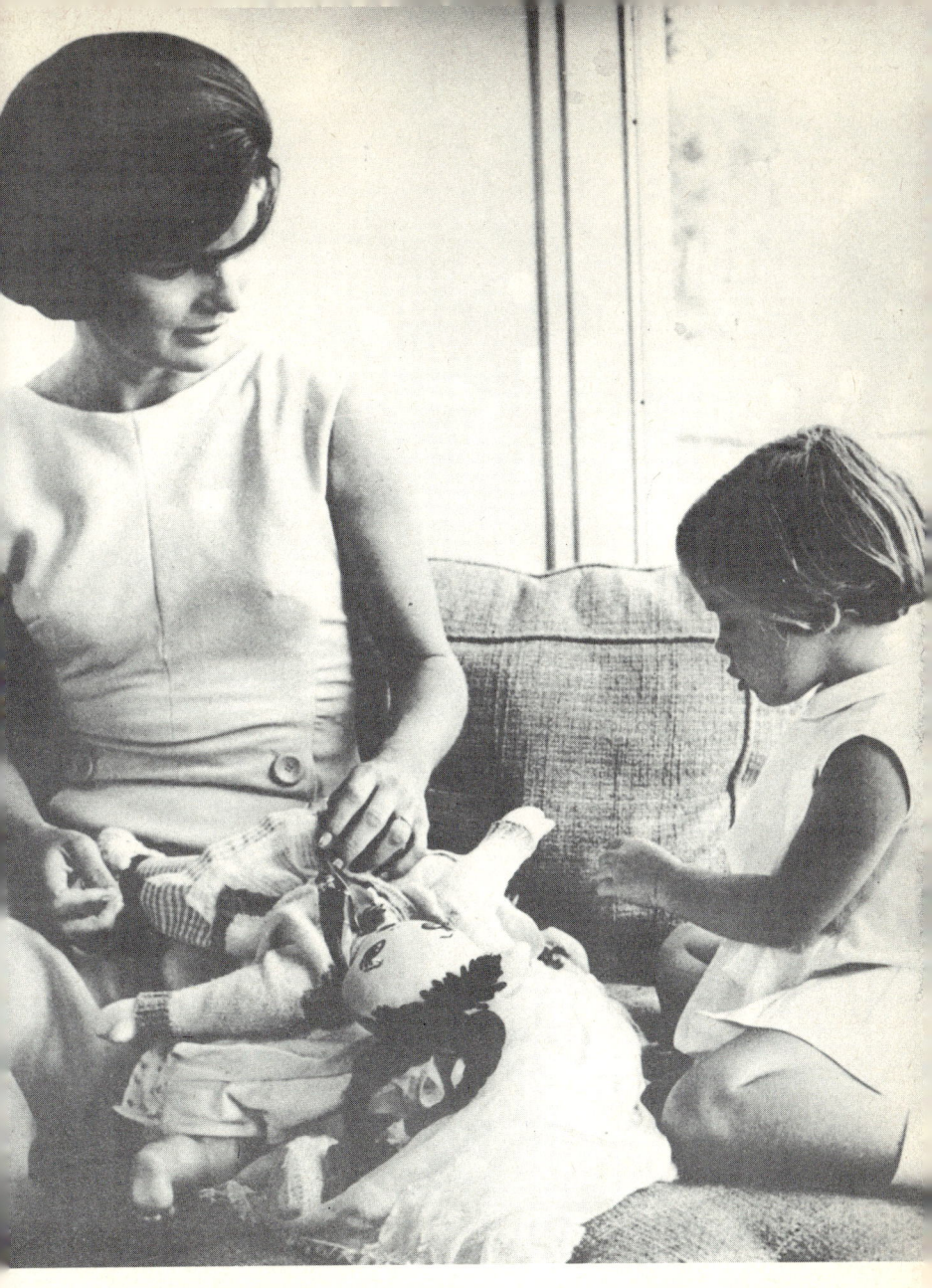

Jackie and Caroline at home together during the lonely campaign months.

November 8, 1960—the final vote was tallied and Americans greeted their new President-elect and his First Lady.

On November 25, 1960, America rejoiced with its new first family over the birth of a son to the President-elect. While Mrs. Kennedy was still in the hospital, Caroline and her "daddy" left their Georgetown home together for Sunday Mass.

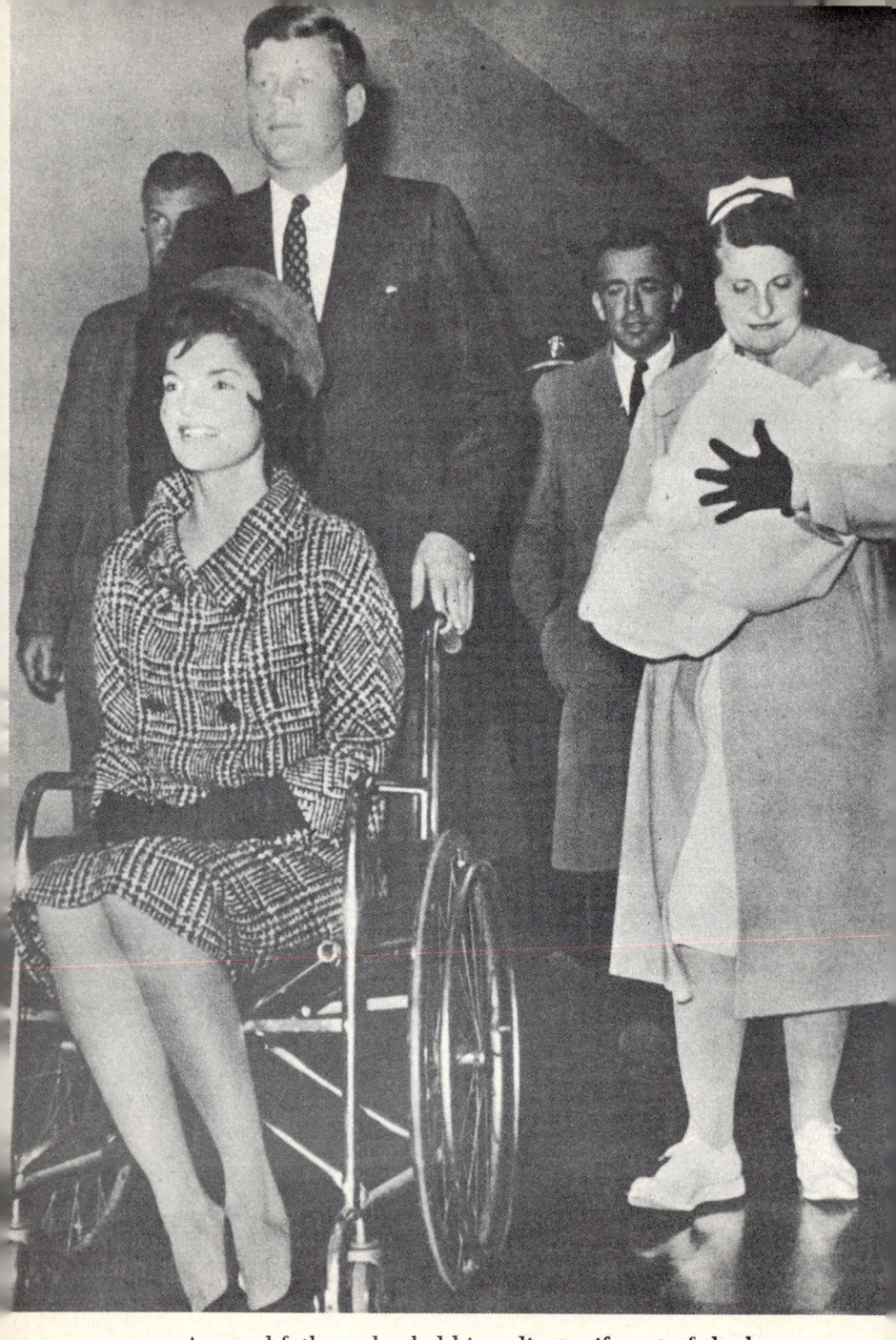

A proud father wheeled his radiant wife out of the hospital, while a nurse carried fourteen-day-old John Junior.

John Junior's Baptism in a Georgetown chapel, under
the gaze of his proud parents.

Caroline welcomes her baby brother.

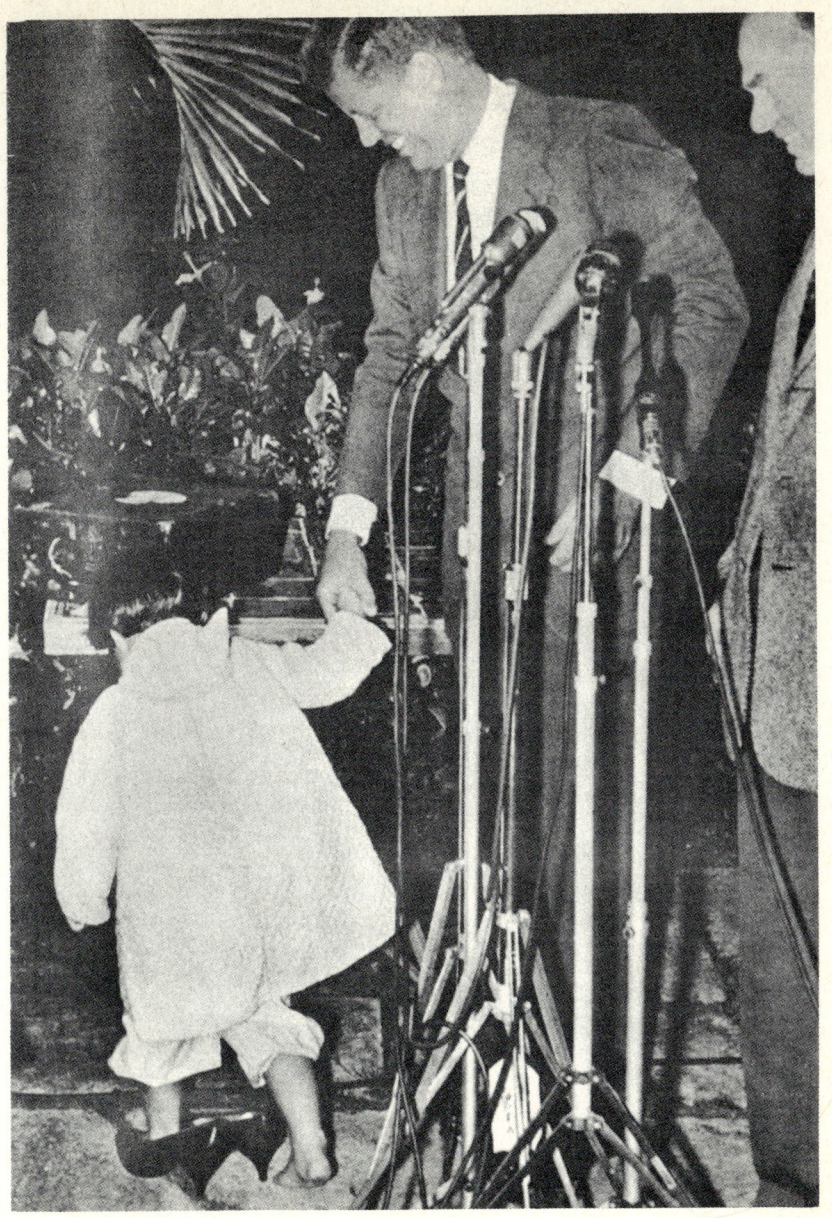

"I want my daddy!" cried Caroline as she burst in on the President-elect's news conference at Palm Beach, in December, 1960.

America's first family moving into the White House.

President John F. Kennedy's Inauguration Day
January 20, 1961

"*Let the word go forth from this time and place to friend and foe alike, that the torch has been passed to a new generation of Americans—born in this century, tempered by war, disciplined by a hard and bitter peace, proud of our ancient heritage—and unwilling to witness or permit the slow undoing of those human rights to which this nation has always been committed.*"

The President and his stunning First Lady off to the Inaugural Ball.

Cardinal Cushing and the guest of honor during the mammoth Presidential Birthday celebration held in Boston, May 30, 1961. The Cardinal Archbishop of Boston, as Robert Kennedy has affirmed, was spiritually closer to John F. Kennedy than any other man.

America's First Lady making a triumphal entrance at Versailles, escorted by President Charles De Gaulle. After the Kennedy's successful trip to Europe, President Kennedy jokingly introduced himself as "the man who accompanied Mrs. Kennedy to Paris."

John John's first birthday picture.

The President of the New Frontier at work, meeting with his Cabinet (above), addressing the nation (below).

"I tell you the New Frontier is here. I believe the times demand invention, innovation, imagination, decision. My call is to the young in heart, regardless of age— to the stout in spirit regardless of Party— to all who respond to the scriptural call: 'BE STRONG AND OF GOOD COURAGE; BE NOT AFRAID, NEITHER BE THOU DISMAYED.' *"*

Innovation, imagination, decision—this is what John F. Kennedy brought to the White House and to America in his thousand days of Presidential leadership, in the form of the Civil Rights Bill, Medicare, international diplomacy, the Nuclear Test Ban Treaty, etc.

(Above) JFK conferring with Russian ministers during the Cuban crisis.

(Right) When he signed the Nuclear Test Ban Treaty John F. Kennedy completed what may some day be considered the most enduring legacy of his administration.

President Kennedy in a familiar pose during a lively press conference.

Astronaut John Glenn showing President Kennedy the Mercury Space Capsule that carried him three times around the globe.

A few moments together, just for each other.

JFK enjoyed watching John Junior fill every day with noisy, bubbling activity.

Mrs. Jacqueline Kennedy planned and presided over White House dinners and receptions with warmth and exquisite grace.

America's First Lady arriving at Fiumicino Airport, Rome, enroute to India for an "official" visit in 1962.

Jacqueline Kennedy at the reception held in her honor at the Quirinal, accompanied by President Gronchi of Italy and his wife.

The following day Mrs. Kennedy was warmly received by His Holiness Pope John XXIII, who showed special interest in her husband and children, and presented her with gifts for them.

After the Papal Audience Mrs. Kennedy traveled to the nearby North American College where she met the Rector, Archbishop Martin J. O'Connor and assisted at Mass in the Seminary chapel.

America's first family leaving church, Easter Sunday morning, 1963.

Two great friends talk together before the opening of
the Boston College Centennial Convocation.

JFK was literally mobbed by admirers at the University of San Diego.

The President and his family visiting historic Gettysburg battlefield. JFK loved to drive but after his election had little opportunity to do so. This outing was one of the last times that he sat behind the wheel.

Immediately after the election of His Holiness, Pope Paul VI to the papal throne, President Kennedy made his historic visit to the Vatican.

Jack and Jackie after a sail, during their last summer together in Hyannisport.

The whole world followed the touching drama of the
death of the President's two-day-old son, Patrick Bouvier
Kennedy. "Farewell, my poor little angel," Mrs. Kennedy
whispered when she was told that her son was dead.
(Above) The President and Mrs. Kennedy leaving Otis Airforce Base Hospital.

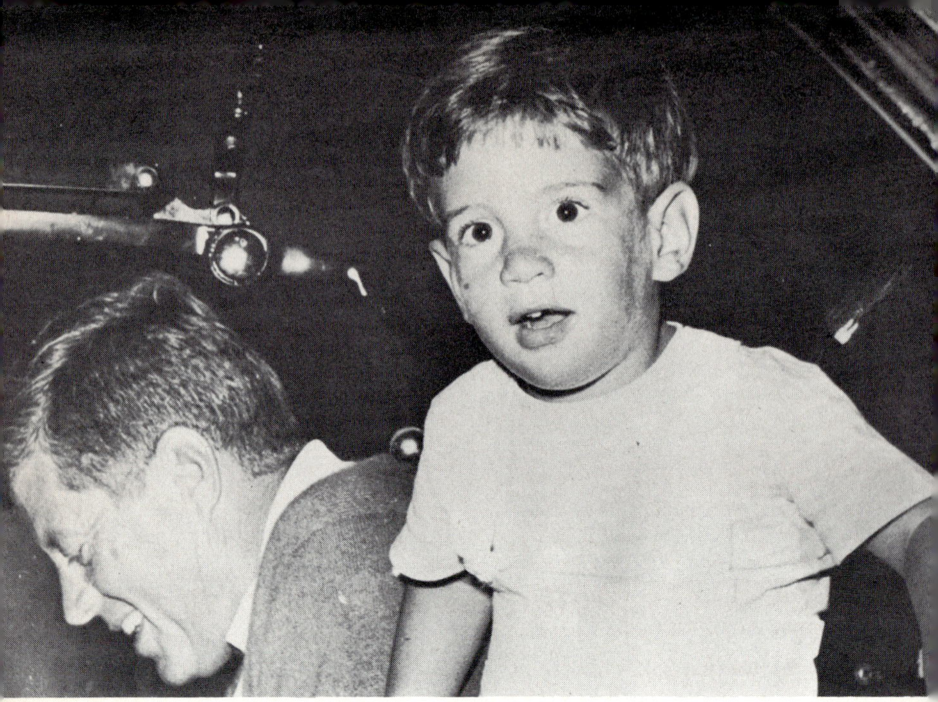

John-John and his "Daddy."

The President and Mrs. Kennedy arriving at Love Field, Dallas, the morning of November 22, 1963. Cheers and outstretched hands greeted the President of the New Frontier.

The Presidential party, accompanied by Governor Connolly, enroute to Dallas.

At 12:30 Dallas time the assassin's shots struck John F. Kennedy. Through the car windshield his arm can be seen in Mrs. Kennedy's white gloved hand.

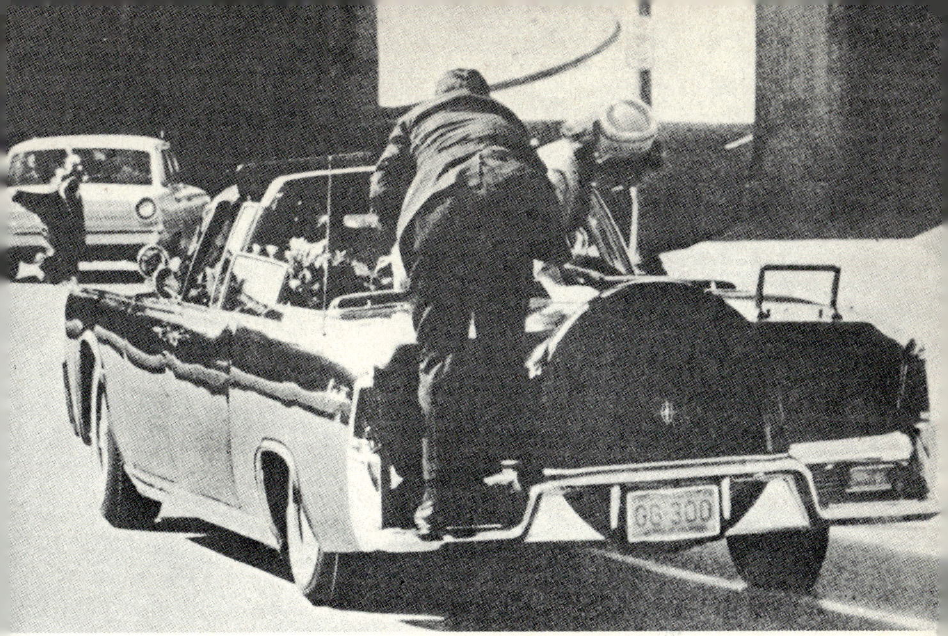

Jacqueline Kennedy rose to her feet in a desperate plea for help. The white arrow points to the slain President's foot, and the black arrow to the wounded Governor Connolly also hit by the assassin. The Presidential car sped immediately to the nearby Parkland Hospital.

Doctors could do nothing for John F. Kennedy. While Jacqueline stood next to her slain husband, Father Huber of Dallas administered the Last Sacraments. Shortly afterward the President's body was carried aboard the Air Force One in a bronze casket. Lyndon B. Johnson was sworn in as the thirty-sixth President of the United States with the widowed Mrs. Kennedy at his side, and the plane winged its way back to Washington.

At Andrews Airforce Base in Washingon, Jacqueline Kennedy, her skirt and legs reddened with her husband's blood, got into the ambulance that was to carry her husband's body to the White House.

A pale yet resolute Mrs. Rose Kennedy on her way to a Mass for her slain son in Hyannisport. When asked if the President's ailing father had been told, she calmly replied, "No, Joe doesn't know yet."

The President's body lying in state in the East Room of the White House, his casket flanked by a military guard of honor.

After a private Mass in the White House and a short period for private family mourning, the President belonged to the sorrowing world. Dignitaries arrived continually at the White House to pay their respects, among them ex-Presidents Truman and Eisenhower, both visibly moved.

On the same caisson which bore the body of
Abraham Lincoln, President Kennedy's body was
carried from the White House to the Capitol building.

In mournful dignity, Mrs. Kennedy, leading Caroline and John-John by the hand, followed the casket as it was carried into the great rotunda of the Capitol.

Mother and daughter kneel beside the casket of a deeply loved husband and father.

A stunned and mourning family listened to the eulogies delivered in honor of the martyred President. Behind Jacqueline Kennedy and Robert Kennedy, were the late Presidents sisters, his brother-in-law Peter Lawford embracing his daughter Sydney, and President Johnson on the extreme left.

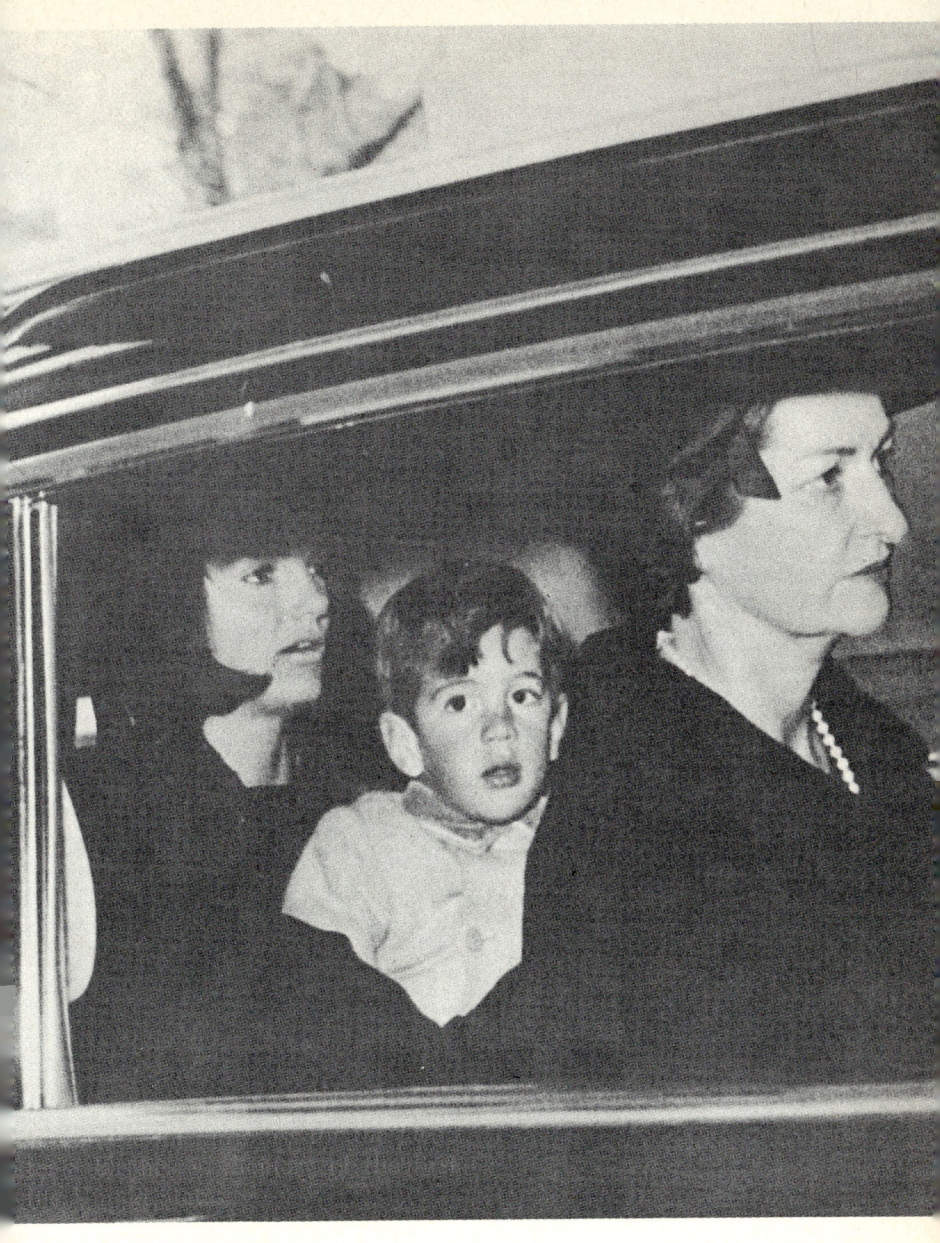

With John-John in her lap, the widowed Mrs. Kennedy returned to the White House accompanied by Mrs. Johnson.

Thousands of mourners in the Washington night waited their turns to file past the coffin of their slain President.

Mrs. John F. Kennedy returned that night to the Capitol rotunda for a brief but sorrowful visit to her husband.

Pope Paul VI assisting at a Solemn Mass for the Dead celebrated in St. Peter's Basilica in memory of the first Catholic President of the United States.

In his touching eulogy, Richard Cardinal Cushing expressed the sentiments of Americans and the world:

"John F. Kennedy has fought the good fight for the God-given rights of his fellow man and a world where peace and freedom shall prevail. He has finished the race at home and in foreign lands, alerting all men to the dangers and hopes of the future, pledging aid in every form to those who were tempted to misinterpret his words, to become discouraged and to abandon themselves to false prophets. He fulfilled unto death the pledge he made on his Inauguration Day: 'I shall not shrink from my responsibilities. . . .'"

The President's casket was placed back on the caisson the morning of November 25th, to be borne past the White House to St. Matthew's Cathedral.

The sad procession leaving the Capitol.

The riderless horse behind the caisson, a mute symbol of the fallen hero.

Mrs. Jacqueline Kennedy and the slain President's brothers following the caisson on foot to St. Matthew's Cathedral. In spite of her heart-rending anguish, Mrs. Kennedy planned and took part in the three day public ceremonies honoring her martyred husband. The courage of this black veiled, valiant woman moved the entire world.

Heads of state from all parts of the world walked in
solemn procession behind the casket of John F. Kennedy.

His Eminence, Cardinal Cushing comforting the President's widow on the steps of the Cathedral.

Leading John-John and Caroline by the hand Mrs. Kennedy entered St. Matthew's Cathedral, followed by Robert, Edward, Mrs. Rose Kennedy and the President's close family.

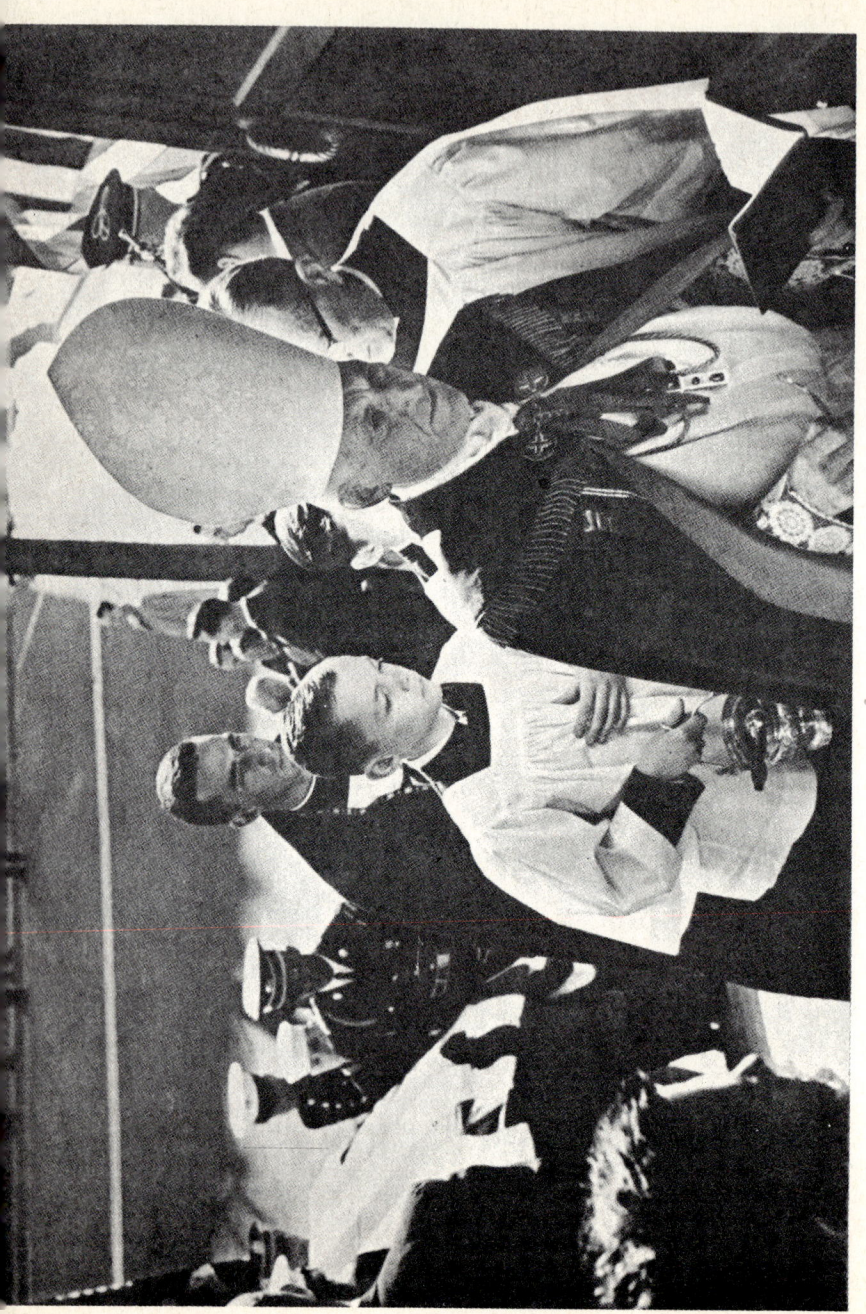

The Cardinal proceeded the casket of "Dear Jack" in a prayerful procession into the Cathedral.

The Funeral Mass for John F. Kennedy celebrated by
Cardinal Cushing.

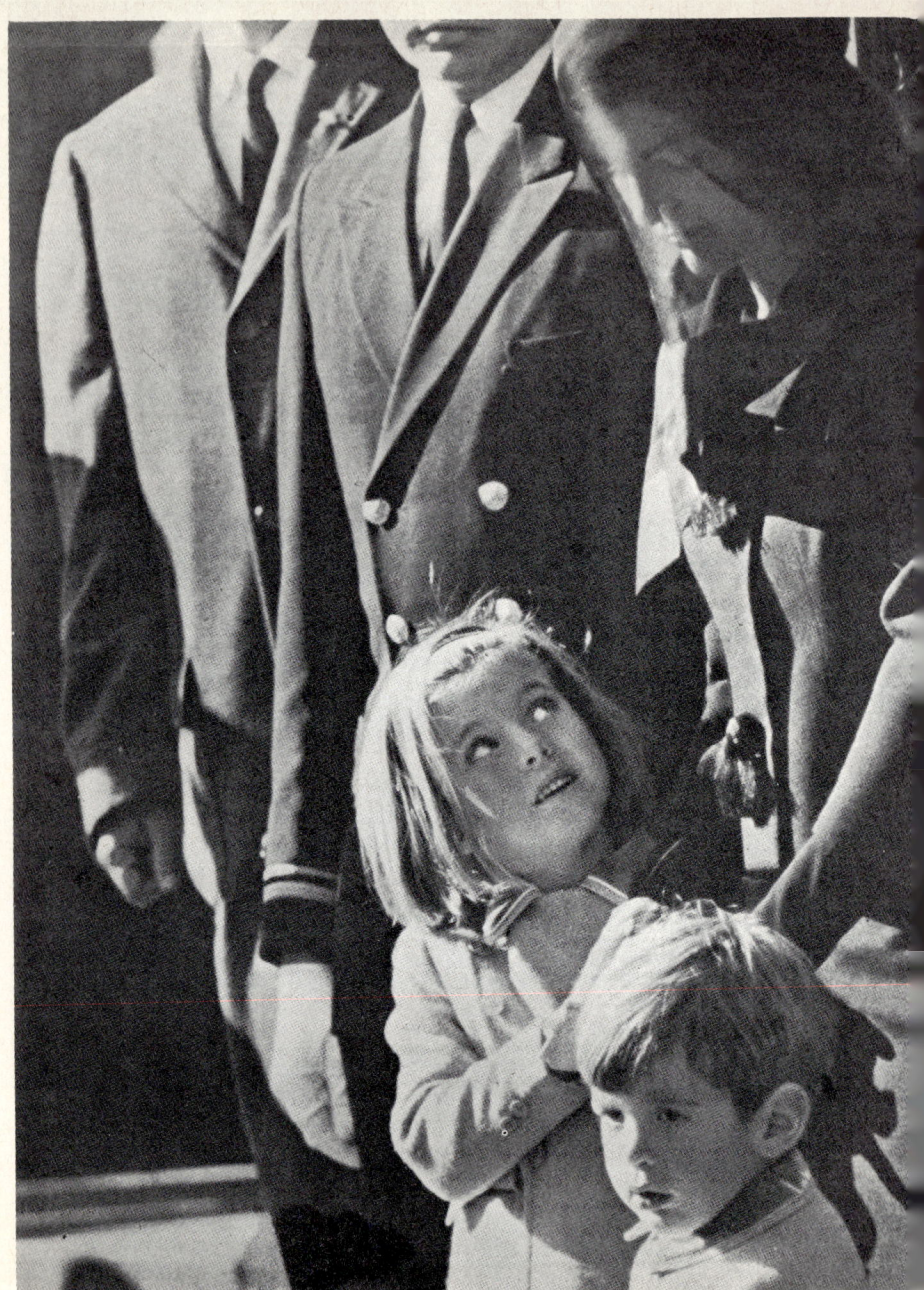

One of the most pathetic scenes in three tragic days: Caroline Kennedy consoling her sorrowing mother. The entire world mourned the death of a head of state but for a small group of people the death of John F. Kennedy meant the loss of a beloved husband, father, son and brother.

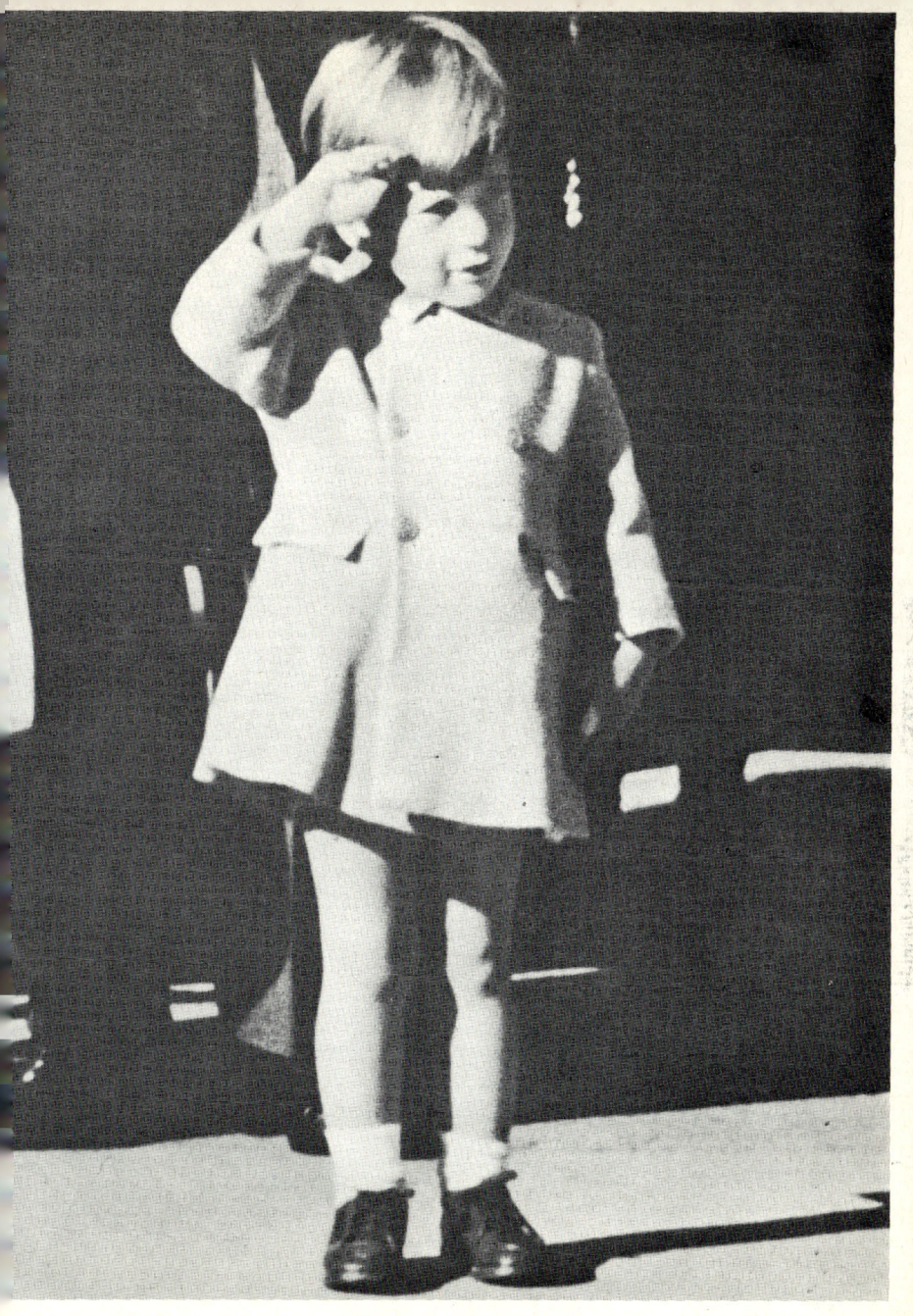

John Junior giving his father a final military salute while the casket was again placed on the caisson. John F. Kennedy, Jr. was three years old the day of his father's funeral.

The funeral cortege passing before the Lincoln Memorial and crossing Memorial Bridge over the Potomic. Beyond the bridge the grassy slopes of Arlington National Cemetery are visible.

The President's casket was gently laid in the open g
moved close with downcast eyes.

while Jacqueline Kennedy, Robert and Rose Kennedy

The final salute and blessing for America's martyred President while Chiefs of State stand at attention. To the right of President De Gaulle is President Luebke of Germany and to his left, Chancellor Erhard.

The Eternal Flame lit by Jacqueline Kennedy burns continually amid flowers and pine boughs. This glowing tribute will be included in the permanent monument to be erected in memory of John F. Kennedy in Arlington.

Clutching the flag which covered her husband's casket, Mrs. Jacqueline Kennedy heard comforting words from Most Rev. Philip M. Hannon of Washington, D.C., who eulogized her husband at the Funeral Mass.

Arlington at night, with the eternal flame glowing in the foreground. The grave of John F. Kennedy has become a national shrine, already visited by over eight million people. On national holidays visitors sometimes number over fifty thousand. After waiting patiently in line, often for hours, they stand a few instants before the President's grave, many murmuring prayers. Some leave affectionate gifts: medals, rosaries, candles. An Indian Chief left his peace pipe, a little girl her First Holy Communion bouquet, an unknown visitor a model of the JFK rocking chair made of flowers.

Along side the grave of John F. Kennedy in Arlington are the graves of two of his children, a baby girl born dead in 1956 and baby Patrick who died after two days of life in 1963.

Jacqueline Kennedy kneeling at her husband's grave. Last May, on the first anniversary of John F. Kennedy's birthday, Mrs. Kennedy took Caroline and John John to Arlington to pray. While there little John entered the white fenced enclosure, bent over his father's flower covered grave and left his precious gift: a metal tie clasp model of the PT 109 that JFK commanded in World War II.

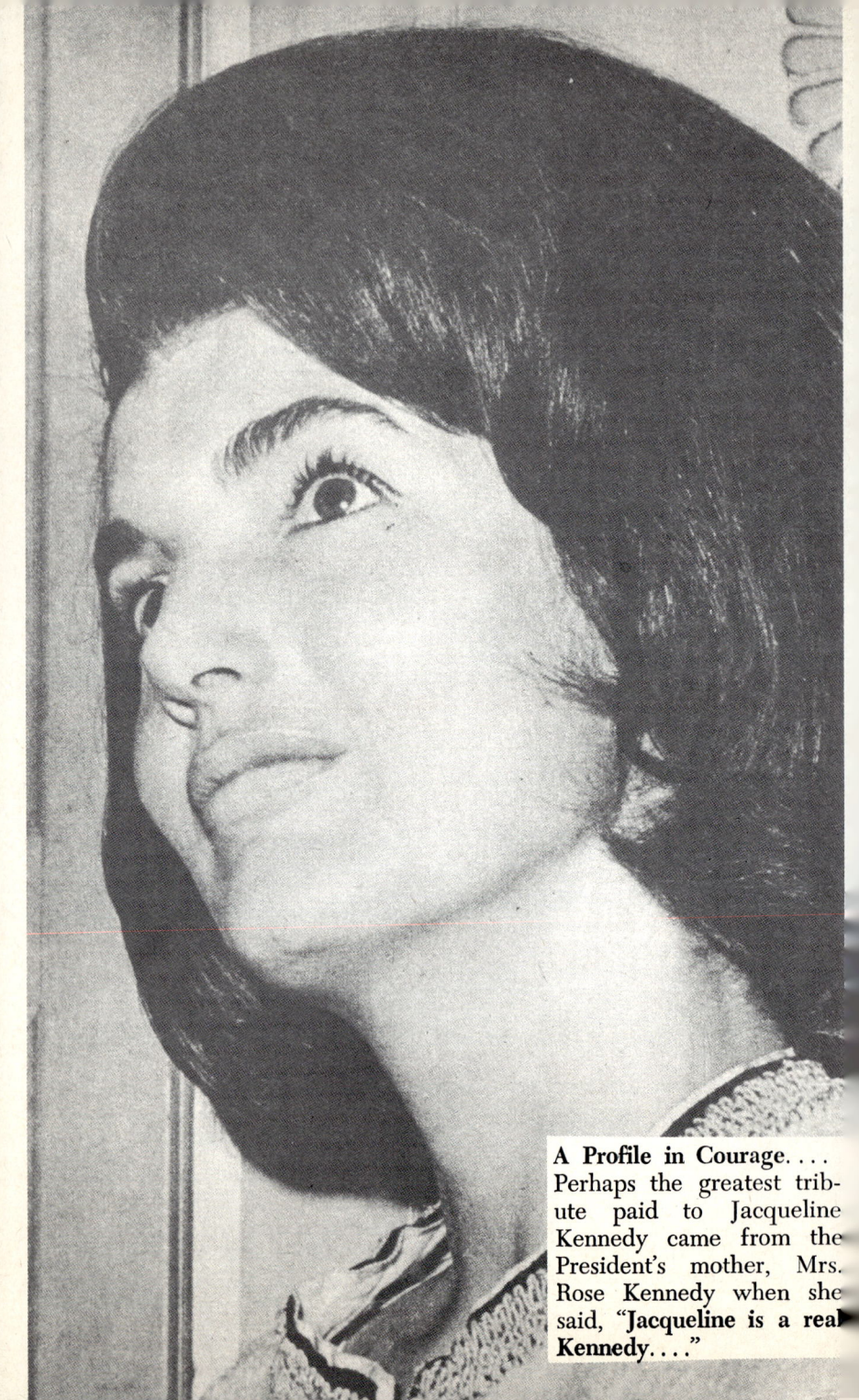

A Profile in Courage....
Perhaps the greatest tribute paid to Jacqueline Kennedy came from the President's mother, Mrs. Rose Kennedy when she said, **"Jacqueline is a real Kennedy...."**

7

COMMANDER IN CHIEF

When a nation spends $51,000,000,000, on the military and defense, more than half its income, the ruler of that armed might is an awesome figure. In the United States the civilian control of the military is absolutely necessary in order to preserve democracy, for the average general is apt to deal only in direct commands, and overlook human values in individuals. JFK deliberately chose Robert Mc-Namara to head the Defense Dept. because he knew how to handle giant corporations.

Kennedy wanted this nation to be so strong that every other nation would be afraid to attack. Since we were determined to pursue peace, this military strength would back up a peaceful policy. But the President was equally determined that waste and inefficiency in the armed forces would be cut to a minimum. The howls of the generals and the admirals were something awful to hear. When it was suggested by some of them that they were naval heroes when JFK was just learning about a PT boat, JFK replied, "But things have changed, now."

And so they had. McNamara handled his 51 billion dollar Pentagon corporation with the same skill he had used when he was President of the Ford Motor Co. Pet congressional projects were cut back, and each new project had to prove its need. Aircraft carriers and manned bombers are rapidly becoming obsolete in an age of missiles and nuclear submarines. The days of the large standing army are also numbered. McNamara demanded cost estimates and cost accounting, and whenever he saw that private industry could produce material cheaper than government installations, he ordered the shutdown of the government base. This did not make him popular with anyone but the President and many tax payers.

Kennedy weathered the storm of congressional disapproval. Frequently the Congressmen who were most vocal in demanding balanced budgets and government economy were the very ones who wanted more defense money spent in their districts and states. Many Senators and Congressmen hold reserve commissions in the Navy or the Air Force, and with this conflict of interest on their records, they often became the spokesman for disgruntled senior officers.

But the President knew that the days of "massive retaliation" were over. No one can win a war in the atomic era. How, then, does a nation face a world in which the only alternatives seem to be annihilation or humiliation? Kennedy searched for another answer. After much reading and research, after a good deal of consideration, he, as commander in chief of the armed forces of the nation, set the policy of "guerilla warfare" and "counter-insurgency" as the alternative.

The Marine Corps and the Army's special forces were to become experts in this type of warfare. Kennedy secured copies of the Cuban communist Ché Guevera's book of guerilla warfare and the writings of Mao Tse-tung and then demanded reports from the American military evaluating the new policy and implementing it. Helicopters and slower, low flying aircraft were brought into training plans for closer ground support. Survival courses were run in the jungles of Panama, on the slopes of the Rockies, and in the deserts.

The Communists had been using infiltration and guerilla tactics successfully for many years. A few American military voices had proposed the program earlier, but Kennedy personally ordered the new policy, and the Marines were the first to experiment with it extensively. Unfortunately, it was too late to use in Laos, the first great problem that JFK had inherited. Kennedy tried hard to bluff the Russians, and eventually they did accede to a type of negotiated peace, but it only gave America a short breathing space.

In the middle of this breathing space, the Bay of Pigs erupted. It was a smashing defeat for a young man who hated to lose. If it weren't so tragic, it could be called a comedy of errors, but men died needlessly because of lack of planning and because of lack of knowledge. Ike had given the signal to the Pentagon and the Central Intelligence Agency to arm Cuban rebels and unleash them on their homeland.

The basic premise was that the Cuban people would rise in revolt as soon as the exiles landed. Everything was planned around that idea. When the moment of truth arrived, the Cuban people did not arise to support the invaders.

When JFK arrived in the White House, he had serious doubts about the invasion. He had been told about it two weeks after his election, and he was very unhappy about the plan. He and Senator Fulbright doubted the morality of such an invasion, but the entire membership of the Chiefs of Staff of the Pentagon assured the new President that it was necessary and feasible. No one was willing to admit the possibility of defeat; no one would tell Kennedy of any flaws in the planning. When JFK insisted that American planes would not bomb Cuba, no one told him that this was the death blow to the plan if the Cubans themselves did not spontaneously take up arms against Castro. The experts assured the President that the invasion would work, so JFK allowed it to continue. Who wanted to appear weak in the face of a Communist threat to the hemisphere?

Castro's intelligence had kept him informed, however, and his men went to work in the United Nations. The image and prestige of the United States was at stake. Were we really to be branded an aggressor before the whole world? Adlai Stevenson had been kept in the dark for security was supposed to be so tight that only the most highly-involved knew anything about it. Kennedy insisted that our military involvement be kept as small as possible so that it would really be a Cuban affair. The only justification JFK could see to permit our engagement was the attempt to "redeem the revolution" that Castro had started, to give the freedom he had promised but never given.

Kennedy had never intended to send in the Marines, and he had made this abundantly clear throughout all the planning. His experts gave him the wrong answers or held back their doubts. While the President accepted the blame for the nation and the world for the disaster, heads had to roll and the

White House organization had to be reshaped. The CIA was given a new director, Bobby Kennedy was brought even more into policy making, and the Joint Chiefs of Staff, old heroes from World War II, were soon to be replaced with younger men who knew that the world had changed.

Did John F. Kennedy make a mistake? The answer is yes. Was it his fault? The answer is no. Added to his youth, idealism, and lack of experience, was his hope for reasonable and negotiated peace between East and West. Beyond all this is the simple fact that the men who should have known did not advise the President properly, especially in view of the fact that his opposition to military intervention was definitely known to the planners. Was the disaster a loss?

In its immediate effects the Bay of Pigs attempt to liberate Cuba was a serious tragedy, but its after effects were more important and beneficial than we can now estimate. First it shocked the President so much that it forced him and Bob Kennedy to re-evaluate their entire attitude toward the presidency itself. It added the fiber of realism and toughness that were to mark the rest of Kennedy's days. Secondly, it left Castro an expense to Russia, a real liability to Communism, and a sword pointed at the Latin American countries, one that would shake them into real anti-Communist activity for the first time. When Cuba did not become a great worker's paradise, the Communist propaganda machine

126   JOHN F. KENNEDY, AMERICAN

throughout Latin America was put on the defensive. If American might had prevailed, this same machine would have stirred up all of the Caribbean area with the lie that Communism would have worked but for the Yankee aggression. America gained more from this "disaster" than we can possibly imagine from this short historical distance.

The American people certainly supported their new President. According to the polls, his popularity shot up to a high of 83% after the crisis, for people admired his sincerity and felt sympathy for him in defeat. Only the professional critics took advantage of the crisis to make remarks and try to take political advantage of him. The successful flight of Alan Sheppard in a rocket in May took some of the attention off the Cuban fiasco, but Khrushchev was also getting ready to force another crisis on the American Commander in Chief.

The Russian leader had never faced Kennedy in an election, or he would not have so underestimated him. The Cuban failure made the Communists contemptuous of JFK's courage, a thing that can never be questioned. In July of 1961, Russia decided to have Berlin. While Kennedy had been rightly hesitant about sending troups to Southeast Asia, thousands of miles beyond reasonable supply routes, and while he had been indecisive about American involvement in Cuba through no deliberate fault of his own, he knew Europe and he was willing to stand firm.

Khrushchev demanded a German peace treaty that would legalize the East German regime. He brought pressure on Berlin and tried to close the access routes. Kennedy started plans for partial mobilization, reinforced the Berlin garrison, and prepared his people for war. There was no wavering, no hesitation. He sent Lyndon Johnson to Berlin to meet the new American troups as they poured into Berlin. When the Russians saw that JFK meant business, the crisis was quietly over.

But not before the Berlin Wall was built. The Communists had to build a wall to keep their people in. It was a tragic admisssion of defeat and Communism has still not recovered fully from the propaganda blow that the Free World levelled against the Wall. It stands as a self-indictment to slavery.

Every president has his critics, and some have had bitter critics. Ordinarily, since this is expected, biographers only take passing notice of the critics, but the almost paranoid fear of Communism that some right wing groups injected into the American system are a real factor in investigating the years of the Kennedy era. Kennedy and his friends became a prime object of their hatred, but Eisenhower, Dulles, the Supreme Court and the United Nations were among other well-known whipping boys. Kennedy, himself, rose above these people, but they helped divide the nation when it needed all its strength to face continuing crisis. It was within this framework that the next crisis came on the world.

For Khrushchev broke the informal moratorium on nuclear testing. The whole world was shocked by this threat to peace. The possibility of contamination of the atmosphere remains a threat to the whole human race and while the scientists may dispute both sides of the question, at present it is a risk that should be unthinkable. But Russia was anxious to make progress in nuclear records and, with the typical Communist contempt for human life, the test began. Kennedy began exercising all the wiles of diplomacy and political persuasion. Pressure was brought particularly through the United Nations. It was to no avail.

Still, the United States was so far ahead in the nuclear arms race that there was no immediate or apparent danger to American security. Kennedy decided to ride it out as long as possible, using to good advantage all the propaganda value that was involved. He held out for months and only when it was demonstrated to him that America might fall behind did he give the word to resume testing. When it was beyond question that the Russian scientists were approaching a new break-through that we could only attain by testing, the risk to all the Free World forced JFK's hand.

With sincere regret he allowed the American scientists to test their atomic weapons in the atmosphere. Every precaution was taken, although that doesn't amount to much. Again, when the Communist leader saw the American determination, he backed down, and the series of events began which led to a nuclear test ban treaty signed by almost every nation in the world, except France and Communist China. This, of course, was many, many months later, but it was one of the first concrete steps toward peace that the world knew since the Korean War. It was typical of President Kennedy's greatness that he always exhausted every possible peaceful means to attain his end before he resorted to a show of strength. He was determined that no war would ever break out "accidentally" because of some hasty and miscalculated act.

In the fall of 1962 the Communists tried again to deceive President Kennedy. They were exploiting their hold in Cuba, a "colony" which was proving very expensive to them. All during the previous summer reports kept filtering in of a Russian build-up in Cuba. The Republicans scented a legitimate political issue and started making campaign noises. Kennedy issued casual denials, partly because there was no definite proof and partly because it did look like simple politics. The extremists took up the cause and started badgering the President. However, without proof, JFK could do little except alert the intelligence agencies to the problem.

Thanks to Doctor Janet Travell, his personal physician, his back was feeling much better, and he entered the political arena again. His youngest brother, Ted, was running for the Senate in Massachusetts, Governor Pat Brown was defeating Dick Nixon for the governorship in California, and there were spirited contests all around the nation. Congress had not been kind to the President, and it is traditional in off-year elections for the "outs" to gain seats. JFK wanted to try to reverse that trend. He simply couldn't afford a more hostile Congress than he had. His tax reform, Medicare program for the aged, war on poverty and civil rights were among many issues at stake.

Only once before had a President reversed the trend and gained seats for his party in a non-Presidential year. That was FDR in 1934. But Kennedy did it. The Democrats won four additional seats in the Senate and only lost two in the House. It was a major victory for the President and showed what solid support he had. If history had gone along its usual course, his party would have lost half a dozen Senators and probably twenty to twenty-five House seats.

But the news of political victory had to wait while the new Cuban crisis really exploded. On October 14, 1962, a high flying U2 plane caught sight of an unusual Russian concentration of technicians and equipment. Examination showed that a missile erector was being put into place. Further pictures and further examination showed work on missiles, missile sites, and more erection equipment. The President knew that there was now no time for peaceful maneuvering. In those first few minutes the whole 1961 Cuban affair flashed through his mind. The mistakes of that event would not happen now.

The team of experts, this time, included Bob Kennedy, Lyndon Johnson, John McCone of CIA, Dean Rusk, Adlai Stevenson, General Maxwell Taylor, Robert McNamara, and a few key aides, such as Ted Sorenson and Pierre Salinger. This time the experts were Kennedy men, people he had chosen and tested, men he could trust implicitly. This time, Kennedy wanted to know everything connected with the crisis, and he wanted to hear all doubts and difficulties.

Security was absolute, this time. During the week of hasty planning and all night meetings, the normal daily routine had to be maintained. Back doors had to be used and simple non-government cars. The current political campaign kept the press corps busier than usual and all of the reporters missed the story—an extremely unusual fact. Ordinarily they would have detected something. Meanwhile, five distinct possibilities were before the President.

He could do nothing and just brave it out. After all, we had missiles in Turkey at the Russian border. He could send the Marines in, but this might involve the Russian soldiers there and force them into war. The Air Force could bomb the sites with their justly famous pin-point bombing techniques. But what about future and more camouflaged sites? An ultimatum could be delivered but would Khrushchev believe it? Finally the blockade was decided upon. While it was technically an act of war, it was more directly aimed at Cuba, could help Khrushchev save face and back down gracefully, and it would leave the President's hands untied for more action, if needed.

The real reason for this Communist action is still somewhat hazy. They might have simply been taking advantage of a situation; they might have been testing Kennedy again for another attempt at Berlin and the German problem. More than likely, from the speed and secrecy of the Russian efforts, Nikita Khrushchev was taking a real gamble to upset the balance of world power in his favor. Had he been successful, the rewards would have been tremendous. If he lost, it would only slow down the Communist drive a little.

After a week of serious and concentrated work, the blockade was determined as the most effective device and the plan was started. Andrei Gromyko was scheduled to return to Moscow to report to the Kremlin on October 21, and he asked to see JFK before he left. When he arrived the talk centered mainly on Berlin, and the Russian was almost belligerent about it. The President casually mentioned

Cuba, but Gromyko shrugged it off. The Soviet deceit was completely proven, and Defense Secretary McNamara started to coordinate the military phase.

That weekend Kennedy went off for his usual campaign tour. In Cleveland and Chicago he addressed huge crowds and asked them to give him a Congress that would support him. But all along the way his mind was on the Cuban affair and he was called so often by Washington to get his advice on the planning, that he knew he had to return. The story was given out that he had a cold and had cancelled the rest of his trip. Even yet, the reporters were not suspicious. The need to surprise the Russians meant that even the American people had to be kept in the dark until the last possible moment.

The security had been complete. Even though a wider and wider circle of people had to be brought into the planning, there were no leaks. Even the wives of the men involved kept the secret! But when JFK returned to Washington and the security was kept tight, the reporters scented something. Word leaked out that some military leaves were cancelled, that a Cabinet meeting was called, and that Congressional leaders were being flown back to Washington. The reporters knew the crisis was here, but not what crisis. When they guessed Cuba, Salinger begged them to give the President time, and they responded magnificently. Not one wrote the story.

During that afternoon, America's allies were told of our plans, the Congressional leaders were briefed (two Southerners dissented and wanted a full fledged invasion) and the Cabinet was formally told. At 5:30 P.M. in Moscow and Washington, the Russians were told, and at 6:00 P.M. the President went on Television to tell the nation, and the world. At 10:00 A.M. on October 24, 1962, the world hovered at the brink of extinction. The quarantine, as the blockade was called, went into effect, and Moscow had the choice of a nuclear holocaust or retreat.

The Navy threw a cordon of ships around Cuba and the Air Force an umbrella of planes over it. The Marines were on board ship and ready for any emergency. San Diego, California was the point of embarkation for West Coast Marines, and the city was practically taken over by them. Florida, Virginia and the Canal Zone took on a wartime look, as well.

Soviet ships were on the high seas headed for Cuba, and Moscow was silent. Plans were made for boarding the ships. The whole world knew that America meant business and held its breath, waiting for the outcome. Bob Kennedy said later, in commenting on these terrible days, that his brother worried most about the children of the world and what might happen to them.

And then the first break came. The Russian ships turned back. The heart of the crisis was over and victory was with the United States. The crisis itself wasn't over that simply, and negotiations between Khrushchev and Kennedy were to go on for several days. Adlai Stevenson and the United Nations played key roles in settling the details, but not before there was an exchange of letters between the Russian leader and the American President. As a face saving demand, Moscow asked assurance that Cuba would not be invaded, but it was a cheap price to pay, and Washington responded in the affirmative. The missiles were withdrawn and peace settled upon the world.

Khrushchev had gambled even greater stakes than he realized. This confrontation with American might and his retreat marked a turning point in world Communism. The Chinese began their open split with Moscow, and other Communist parties began to show some independence, using Khrushchev's "softness" with the West as their excuse. Some day, historians may date the close of the Russian Marxist Revolution as the day on which Kennedy placed the whole might of America on the line before Khrushchev and said, "Don't take another step."

That doesn't mean that a permanent and lasting peace has come upon the world. There are still crises in the world and grave problems. The future of China may make it the nuclear "tiger" of the next generation, but the world has faced nuclear war and turned back, and the time now granted to the human race must be used to further the cause of peace and justice, or there may not be another chance. John Fitzgerald Kennedy was the instrument of Divine Providence in giving us this chance.

8

"MY FELLOW AMERICANS"

The Kennedy years involved much more than the record of foreign affairs, important as that was. On the home front there were problems of such magnitude that, at one time, it looked as if civil war might break out. There was also the day to day running of the country, a task of complex magnitude. As the country grows in population and wealth, the functions of government grow, too.

The intimate life of the Kennedy family also grew apace, with Caroline beginning school and "John-John" going through the cutest phase of his infancy. When the President's back felt all right, there were occasional rounds of golf. The presidential yacht, the Honey Fitz, was often in use in good weather and almost daily the President found time for a swim in the White House swimming pool. The rocking chair that Dr. Travell prescribed became a national symbol and the furniture manufacturers said that when Kennedy started to use one, their sales went up almost one thousand per cent.

The President took his campaign promises seriously, and one of the first that he started to fulfill was the glamorous idea of the Peace Corps. When he announced his plan about a month before his election, the idea was ridiculed by his enemies, yet it turned out to be one of the most successful of his projects and today, no one doubts its effectiveness.

The Peace Corps was a bold venture in which the President invited young Americans to give a year or two of their lives to the underprivileged of the world, to share their blessings as Americans with people who had no such traditions to spur them on. His brother-in-law, Sargent Shriver, was put in charge of the program, and from the first it was swamped with volunteers and calls for help from foreign governments.

The corpsmen are selected only after rigorous investigation and then subjected to an equally rigorous training. They go to live in the backland villages of Africa, Asia and South America. They live with the natives and like the natives, while they train them in basic agriculture to raise living standards, basic hygiene to cut down disease, and start simple elementary schools to combat ignorance. Their pay is only a small honorarium and, as long as the military draft continues, they are still subject to it. It is a life of heroism and sacrifice, but it is an independent contribution to the freedom of mankind and the elevation of the human spirit.

The space program also met with the general approval and support of the nation. When Kennedy espoused the program, the country was at least ten years behind the Russians. With sufficient money and moral support, the American scientists were able to cut that gap in half, and then cut it again, until by the end of his life JFK knew that we were up to the Communists in some fields, and ahead of them in others. The Astronauts themselves were the finest young men that America could offer, and NASA, the agency in charge of the space race, proved itself capable and efficient. Alan Sheppard's space flight was soon followed by Marine Colonel Glenn's three-orbit flight, and the space program continued to make giant strides.

Life on the New Frontier settled into a relaxed and homey daily routine, with long hours of work leading to the enjoyment of the family circle. John Kennedy always took time to look in on Jackie and the children during the day, and when he left the office at night it was to retire to the family quarters. Dining out became less fashionable in government circles, as did the constant round of cocktail parties. Kennedy expected his officials to be on the job early, promptly, and clear of mind and eye. Occasionally the Kennedys would go to the theater or a small dinner party. Frequently they would have the family or close friends in, for a quiet dinner. When Jackie did have a big party, it was always a success and always in good taste.

Jackie had trained the President to look neat and well-groomed, a feat that neither his mother nor Choate had been able to do. The rest of the staff followed suit, although Pierre Salinger probably held out the longest. The New Frontiersmen were an intellectual group, most of whom had written important books. They were at home in the world of culture, music and the arts. Jackie scored one of the big social upsets when she had Pablo Casals, the eighty-year-old world famous cellist, entertain the cream of Washington's leaders. Great men and women in the cultural world were often invited, as well as old friends from the days before the campaign for the presidency.

Formal state dinners were held as protocol directed, but the world famous leaders for whom they were given would be entertained informally before or after almost as part of the family. Kennedy made no secret of his simple tastes or his delight at having his children around him, as well as his nieces and nephews. He enjoyed the Marine Corps band and looked forward to seeing it at any function. Neither did he hide his delight at the song "Hail to the Chief" which is reserved for the President. Travel, too, remained an important part of his schedule and a trip to New York or Florida was as casually arranged as a drive to the Justice Department. He almost always looked forward to the press conferences.

And so, despite the many crises that surrounded him, the wholesome family life in the White House was a joy to the American people, and an example to them. At one time, three of the Kennedy wives were expecting—Jackie, Mrs. Robert Kennedy and Mrs. Edward Kennedy. Unfortunately, Jackie gave birth prematurely to Patrick Bouvier Kennedy, who died after forty hours of life. This was a hard blow for the first family, and the nation suffered with them.

There seemed to be no end to the things that interested the President. He fought for the conservation of the country's natural resources and its National Parks. He worked for programs for the mentally retarded. During his administration the first national legislation was passed to strengthen the country's libraries. The list seems really endless.

But some of his interests brought him into bitter struggles.

In two areas on the domestic front, the very vitality of the nation is most at issue: farmers and laborers. In agriculture there are no easy answers for there are so many variable factors not under man's control. Yet Kennedy's sincere interest in the farmer can never be questioned and he tried to keep farm prices stable and surpluses under some sort of control. For the working man, there must be job security, decent wages and working conditions, and as little inflation as possible.

Steel prices are usually the key to inflation, for it is so basic an item in modern civilization that it sets the trend for all prices. If steel prices are raised $5.00 a ton, automobile prices may go up $50.00. If wages then have to be renegotiated, an inflationary spiral starts which can be increasingly difficult to control, or stop. In the fall of 1961, Kennedy and his efficient Secretary of Labor, Arthur Goldberg (now a Supreme Court Justice), had entered into the steel labor contract making, and had finally persuaded the union to drop its demands for a wage increase and be satisfied with increased fringe benefits. The steel industry was making the best profits in its history, outside of war time, and could absorb the cost of the benefits.

In April of 1962, however, the Chairman of the United States Steel Corporation, Mr. Roger Blough, called Ken O'Donnell's office late one afternoon and asked if he could come over to see the President. Besides Blough's important position, he was also chairman of the President's Business Advisory Council. The business community is usually Republican and had supported Nixon against JFK, so Kennedy was trying to woo business support. All told, Blough was told to come over.

Blough had come to tell the President that U.S. Steel Corp. had raised its prices $6.00 a ton. He gave the President a copy of a news release. Kennedy sent for Secretary Goldberg who arrived in less than ten minutes. Kennedy controlled his anger well, but Goldberg, a former top union lawyer exploded. Six months earlier Blough had used the good offices of the President and the Labor Department to obtain a favorable labor contract. Now he was taking advantage of it to raise prices and start a dangerous inflationary curve. He would not listen to the President but was simply unbending in his decision to have this price increase.

After he left, JFK paced his office furiously. Then he set the wheels in motion to fight back, for not only his prestige as a President was at stake, but his very manliness. He could not knuckle under to such a raw betrayal of the working man by big business. Bobby Kennedy came in, Clark Clifford, Secretary of the Treasury Douglas Dillon, Sorenson, O'Donnell and Salinger. The whole team was mustered for battle. David McDonald, the president of the steel worker's union was called in. When five other steel firms joined in the price rise within hours, making almost 85% of the industry in all, the lines were drawn for the fight. Defense Secretary Robert McNamara was to be at the center of the Kennedy strategy, since the Pentagon placed most of the steel orders on all government contracts.

Anti-trust suits could be sought from the courts, but this would be a matter taking months to decide and immediate action was needed. Senator Gore and Senator Kefauver offered to push bills through Congress regulating prices, but Kennedy did not want a managed economy which is always dangerous to free enterprise. Walter Heller, the economic advisor in the White House, began gathering facts and and figures for Kennedy to put before the American people. Lyndon Johnson acted as executive officer to the battle group.

Within forty-eight hours of the announcement Heller came to the group with these figures. Inland Steel in Chicago had held out on the steel industry and kept its prices down. With them and some smaller companies, 16% of the steel industry were with the President, temporarily, at least. Immediately McNamara announced that a five and a half million dollar steel contract was being awarded to these smaller companies. With what the government would need in the near future, 25% of the steel production could be channeled to these companies. The larger companies would lose about 10% of their business in the immediate future. When it is realized that even a one percent change can mean hundreds of millions of dollars to so basic and huge an industry, it became obvious where the government's pressure must come.

Kennedy kept the country constantly informed of what was going on, and an aroused public opinion backed the President. When the President went to keep a weekend appointment with the Navy, reviewing naval maneuvers and a Marine Corps landing, the White House staff turned the full power of the government's purchasing practices toward the steel crisis. Before JFK had finished inspecting the first nuclear submarine, Bethlehem Steel, the country's second largest, announced a price roll-back. By the time Kennedy boarded a cruiser to put out to sea, U.S. Steel had surrendered, and the crisis was over.

The exuberance that had marked the transition of power to the Kennedy administration was long since gone. In those early days when a family member might be playfully shoved into the swimming pool at an out-door party, the mood had been one of youth glorying in its sense of purpose and its sense of challenge. But the challenges had come so fast and so furious, that whenever there was breathing space, it became a treasured time of relaxation. The new administration had grown up in power and maturity and it exercised both with prudence and wisdom.

But the Civil Rights struggle, which almost turned into civil war, tested every ounce of endurance that the Kennedy forces could muster. It wasn't a weekend crisis over steel prices, or a two week journey to the brink of war. It was a constant pressure, a nerve-racking, persistent and dangerous situation that faced the conscience of the whole nation. The American Bishops in their national pastoral in 1958 and in 1963 called it basically a moral and religious struggle.

Pope John XXIII, in his great encyclical PACEM IN TERRIS had explored the whole subject of human rights. He called upon civil government to give special attention to the rights of minorities. He urged all men to work to secure their civil rights. The Pope wrote, "Racial discrimination can in no way be justified," and he based his arguments on the natural law, the words of Christ, and the principles of justice and charity.

Indeed, the whole American dream is based on the fact that there are certain self-evident truths which support the claim of every individual to his personal, human, and civil rights. The equality of each human being is enshrined in the basic documents of the American democracy, from the Declaration of Independence to the Constitution and the Bill of Rights. These were enforced by the Emancipation Proclamation and the Fourteenth Amendment to the Constitution.

With the ideals expressed by the founding fathers of the nation, it seems incredible that the horrible blot of slavery could ever have been accepted in America. After the terrible struggle of the Civil War, it seems equally incredible that a century after President Lincoln the condition of the Negro American was little better than that of economic slavery, with few exceptions. For a hundred years the Negro citizen waited patiently for his rights, for good education for his children, equal opportunity for jobs, voting and housing. Has ever a race suffered so silently and so long? Would not even the patience of holy Job be finally exhausted?

Many other minority groups, particularly the Mexican American and the Puerto Rican, suffered similar indignities. Racial and religious discrimination have often rocked America, and Jews and Catholics, Irish, Italian and Polish minorities have felt the lash of hatred. But the Negro has a mark, color, which never permits him to hide anonymously in the big city or on the farm while he waits out the hatred, improves himself, and "passes" as a native American.

Kennedy sensed that the time for real "emancipation" had arrived. Intellectually and morally he was ready for it, desired it, longed for it. The unrest within the colored community could no longer be held back and even if his re-election were put in jeopardy, this was a crusade with a high and noble purpose, and there was no turning back. Bobby Kennedy was one with his brother in this resolve.

Civil Rights demonstrations had begun with full force in late 1960, and a week before the election, John Kennedy tried to help the great Negro leader, Martin Luther King, when he was arrested following a sit-in in the Deep South. Extreme right-wing groups accused the Communists of infiltrating the movement simply to stir up trouble, but Kennedy knew that the only answer to this was that American and Christian leadership must channel the energy of the movement into positive and constructive acts. If Christians are found wanting in this moral crusade, they surrender the cause of justice to the Reds, and have only themselves to blame.

One of the first executive orders issued by John F. Kennedy after his election was to establish the Committee on Equal Employment Opportunity under the capable direction of Lyndon Johnson. Johnson's view of civil rights corresponded to the American national ideal. His commitment to civil rights was sincere dedication.

If a selfish view of this struggle were the only one taken, it would still be to the advantage of the country to promote equal rights for all citizens. Economically, if the people of minority groups are put to work productively, they increase the wealth of the nation, put more money into circulation, create new jobs, and bolster the strength of the nation. On the diplomatic level, the whole world must watch

the "American Experiment." If we preach the benefits of democracy to the world, then we must expect
the world to watch us critically.

The emerging nations of Africa and Asia will
not trust us, if they find that minorities in this country, related to them by race or religion, are perse-
cuted or repressed. And only the Communists can
benefit from a situation of legitimate unrest and
injustice. Selfishly speaking, civil rights makes sense.
Morally speaking, the Christian has no choice, for
Christ has given the command to "love our neighbor
as ourselves." There is no alternative for the follower
of Christ. And John Fitzgerald Kennedy was a sincere Catholic, a man who knew the will of God and
practiced fraternal charity.

Under Kennedy, Negroes found that they had
equal opportunity in competition for any position
in the Federal government. The assistant press secretary was the competent and courteous Andrew
Hatcher, and federal judgeships, state department
jobs, ambassadorial positions and United Nation appointments were open to, and impartially filled by
competent men of every race of Americans.

The growing unrest broke out in demonstrations
throughout the Deep South, and the nation and the
world were shocked to see "Bull" Connor, the police
chief of Birmingham, Alabama, turn fire hoses, police dogs, and cattle prods on peaceful demonstra-
tors. Little Negro churches were bombed and
burned, and one Sunday morning girls at Sunday

School were the victims of a bombing attack. The local and state police officials turned a deaf ear to pleas for help. This callous disregard for human values and human life went right up to the State Capitols and Governors' Chairs in most southern states.

Kennedy ordered the Justice Department to enforce the civil rights bills that Congress had passed, even though they had been weakened by Southern filibusters. It soon became evident that the Federal government was limited in the work it could initiate in the Civil Rights field. Kennedy would have preferred to wait until after his re-election to start a new civil rights legislation battle with Congress, because then he would be in a stronger position. But the Negro would not wait, could not wait, and after the bitter struggle in Mississippi in September 1962, the administration went to work to prepare a strong bill to present to Congress when it reconvened in 1963.

Bob and Jack Kennedy felt that the key to the struggle must center around voting rights and education. If the Negro were free to exercise his rights in these two fields, he could improve himself and finally come to full stature as a citizen. The unions had to be encouraged to accept and train Negro apprentices and fair housing and equal opportunity laws must be supported. Senator Goldwater and the extreme conservatives screamed that this was an invasion of State's Rights, that the Federal government had no power in these fields. The liberal and

Christian forces replied that the Negro had waited a century for the State to act, and many of them never would. How much chance would civil rights legislation have in the legislature of Mississippi or Alabama? As for the Federal government's right, not only was there the Fourteenth Amendment, but there was the whole philosophy of the entire American system, dedicated to the principles of human dignity.

The tragedy at Oxford, Mississippi in 1962 finally triggered the opening of the civil rights direct-involvement by the Kennedy team. Before that it had been mostly a moral commitment and the regular enforcement procedures of Bob Kennedy's Justice Department. But now James H. Meredith, a veteran of nine years in the Air Force, wanted to finish his college education. This was not too unusual. American Negroes had distinguished themselves in every branch of the service. JFK had seen Negro Marines storm ashore under enemy fire in the South Pacific. And many of these colored service men returned home to go to college, although they knew they might still end up as janitors or garbage collectors. But James Meredith wanted to go to the University of Mississippi.

Southerners have masked the enforcement of segregation under a doctrine of "separate but equal" facilities, including schools, even as Northerners have turned their backs on the equivalent discrimination of segregated slum areas. The cry of the Negro throughout the land in the 1960's was "Freedom Now!" And James Meredith wanted to go to the University of Mississippi.

Nowhere in the nation was there so closed a society as in Mississippi. Even Alabama had made some protests but also some progress. Governor Wallace of Alabama seemed more interested in making political progress for himself than any other thing in his petty drama of standing in the schoolhouse door. If the Northern steel industries which controlled business in Birmingham really wanted to force integration peacefully, they could. So far they have not. But Mississippi was determined to remain "lily white!"

On the evening of October 2, 1962, Federal Marshals, armed with court orders, arrived at the campus of the University of Mississippi in Oxford. Nick Katzenbach, a Justice Department deputy waited inside the Lyceum Building to command the operation, with an open telephone to the White House. Outside, General Edwin Walker, a former Army commander who had been admonished for his ultra-right wing activities, was addressing a mob that grew steadily more ugly.

Governor Ross Barnett had called earlier to beg the President to keep Meredith out. He cried that he couldn't protect the young man. JFK strode to the phone and shouted "Get your State Police on that campus. You fulfill your duty as governor and keep the peace." Barnett did nothing. The State Troopers were strangely absent. Barnett wanted to force the President to use federal force so that he would be absolved of blame. Kennedy wanted the whole nation to get the true picture.

The Kennedy brothers refused to call out the soldiers. Instead, they used federal peace officers, a force consisting of 500 Federal Marshals. The plan had been for the State Troopers to handle the crowds while the federal court orders were served and enforced. Instead, the troopers disappeared at the most critical time and a riot formed. Tear gas was used, the crowd fired at the Marshals, and a newsman was killed. Finally, JFK had to call out the National Guard. He did so reluctantly, because once again, the whole world saw only that it took federal bayonets to get civil rights for an American citizen if he were a colored man. And the Communists distributed thousands of pictures of the event all over Africa and Asia.

The critics pounced on Kennedy, of course. Right wing organizations tried to make a hero out of Walker. They would have tried with Barnett, too, but he had proved himself so unreliable that they didn't dare. A local grand jury even tried to indict the Federal Marshals as the cause of the riot! Kennedy had tried to use every legal and peaceful means at his disposal. He had trusted his fellow Americans to use good sense, but at the last moment the Americans at "Old Miss" acted more like Nazis than Americans.

However, once Meredith was in the university, peace slowly returned, and men of good will across the nation and in the South as well, had to admit the sincerity of JFK's purpose and his strength of will. It was a major victory for integration and set the stage for a new and stronger Civil Rights Bill. Bob Kennedy and his staff, with key congressional people like Senator Hubert Humphrey, went to work on a new bill that was to be presented to the new Congress when it met in 1963.

On February 28, 1963, John Kennedy sent a special message to Congress detailing the need. He started with a quote from Justice Harlan at the turn of the century, "Our Constitution is color blind and neither knows nor tolerates classes among citizens." The President pointed out that this might be true in theory, but nowhere in the country, North or South, East or West, was it put into practice entirely. He went on:

"The negro baby born in America today has about one-half as much chance of completing high school as a white baby born in the same place on the same day—one third as much chance of completing college—one third as much chance of becoming a professional man—twice the chance of unemployment—one seventh as much chance of earning $10,000 a year—a life expectancy which is seven years less—and the prospects of earning only half as much."

He pointed out that a century had elapsed since the Emancipation Proclamation yet the minority races still suffered economic and social deprivation. He publicly examined the evils of discrimination, offered reasons for improving the situation, and ended up his introduction by saying that true equality of opportunity must be given to all and "The basic reason is because it is right."

The first section of his message then asked for protection of voting rights. He asked for power to appoint federal voting referees wherever there was suspicion of fraud, for a speed-up of judicial action on voting cases on the theory that "Justice delayed is Justice denied," and he asked power for the Justice Department to initiate action when necessary. He urged the passing of the 24th Amendment which would outlaw poll taxes. He asked that special tests and special literacy examinations for minority races be outlawed.

Since the area of education was so vital to equality of opportunity, he asked that special aid be given to school districts that were desegregating. The Federal Civil Rights Commission had to be strengthened and in the field of employment more opportunities had to be provided for qualified members of minorities, racial or religious. The most controversial part of his message dealt with public accomodations. No longer should Negroes be kept from restaurants, motels, theaters, stores, and the like. Whenever private enterprise opens its doors to the public, it must serve the public, not segments of it on the unjust basis of race, color or creed.

John F. Kennedy was very strict in the use of Federal funds on projects that might practice discrimination. He told Congress that he had issued Executive Orders prohibiting discrimination in any housing financed in whole or in part with federal funds. The Justice Department was ordered to investigate charges of police brutality, and the Armed Forces were again reminded of the orders barring discrimination in Reserve forces and in civilian work hiring programs.

The President asked Congress for real progress in the civil rights crusade. He reminded them that we can't legislate morality, but we can protect those who are discriminated against, and give them recourse to law for the redress of grievances. Real progress of a positive nature must come from the hearts and minds of men, recognizing the God-given equality of rights in the human person.

As we saw before, the President had hardly finished the message before the hue and outcry began. JFK had asked for such a strong bill that everyone expected a weakened compromise. The conservatives who denied that the government had the right to enter this field were the same people who fought local fair housing and equal opportunity laws in their home states and cities. They were the same people who supported so-called "right to work" laws, designed to hurt the labor unions.

They immediately planned to team up with the cynical Southern Senators, who were already drawing up plans for a filibuster. They bottled up the bill in key committees, called long lines of witnesses, and tried to brow beat Bob Kennedy when he was on the stand. They even added stronger provisions to the bill, so that the moderates and middle-of-the-road legislators would vote against it. President Kennedy didn't live to see the bill passed, but it did.

More than likely, it took his death to get so strong a bill through Congress. After his death, Bobby Kennedy said to Congress, "My brother's heart and soul are in that bill." Lyndon Johnson told them, "This bill must pass as a living memorial to John Fitzgerald Kennedy." And so the strongest Civil Rights Bill ever to pass Congress went on the books; now JFK's "fellow Americans" must make it work. It certainly ranks with the Test Ban Treaty as one of the most important acts of his fruitful career.

9

A 21st CENTURY MAN

Time was running out for President Kennedy but no one could foresee that. He was busily making plans in mid-1963 for the campaign for re-election. He knew he needed a great mandate from the people, even a landslide victory, if the program of the New Frontier was to succeed. One of the things that plagued him most was the way Congress stalled on the Medicare program.

Millions of America's senior citizens were in need of medical care and hospitalization at the very time in their lives that they could least afford it. Kennedy wanted nothing to do with socialized medicine. The Kennedy program called for uniting a type of basic medical insurance with social security, which is a type of retirement insurance. Neither is fully an insurance program because the government must put in funds to underwrite the program, but it is a wise and progressive use of tax money.

Kennedy also had to look forward to the defense of the hemisphere and Western Europe. Relations with Canada and Mexico had to be maintained and improved. His visit to Mexico was triumphant, and millions of the people there lined the road shouting "Viva el Catolico" as he made a pilgrimage to the shrine of Our Lady of Guadalupe. There was a meeting in Nassau in the Bahamas with the British Prime Minister to propose a multilateral nuclear force for the NATO countries.

Charles De Gaulle of France, unfortunately, longed for the good old days of French nationalism, and he blocked the military alliance, as well as Britain's entrance into the European Common Market. Kennedy felt that this would be one of the most important problems of his new administration—the management of De Gaulle. The great French general had undoubtedly saved France twice, but his vision stopped early in the twentieth century, and JFK was already planning for the next century.

The foreign aid program was in trouble, and ex-Marine David Bell was put in charge. Kennedy wanted the entire concept of foreign aid re-examined and improved. Self-help programs must be given priority; our friends must be helped; democracy must be promoted around the world; and, the strong nations of Europe must start to do their share. Bob Kennedy was sent to Brazil to talk government reform and Jack, himself, went to central America to meet with their six Presidents, to promote the Alliance for Progress.

In the face of a big budget deficit, JFK wanted a tax cut immediately, and tax reform for the near future. The theory is that if the economy grows, even a reduced tax revenue will grow also and more than make up the difference. While a balanced budget is always desirable, deficit spending by government is always manageable, for authorizations and appropriations are always years ahead of the actual outlay of money.

With the approach of summer, Kennedy longed to get out and meet the people. Too long a stay in Washington at any one time always left him feeling somewhat bored and frustrated. In three years in office, the lines had grown in his face and the gray had begun to creep into his hair. His back, always in precarious condition, gave him little peace.

It was at this time that someone pointed out to him an old order of President Theodore Roosevelt, ordering the Marines to take 50 mile hikes.

Kennedy met the Marine Corps Commandant, General David Shoup, and kidded him about the condition of the average Marine of 1963. This caught the imagination of the nation, and not only were Marines out hiking, but Bobby Kennedy, members of the administration, and clubs everywhere started it. Finally the doctors had to caution those in less than top physical condition. The clincher came when the portly Pierre Salinger tried to make the hike. He made only six miles of it and gave up, explaining "I may be plucky, but I am not stupid."

Birmingham again exploded in civil rights violence, and the movement spread from city to city throughout the South. Bob Kennedy hurried to New York to meet with such Negro leaders as James Baldwin, Lena Horne, and Harry Belafonte, only to come away shocked at the bitterness he discovered in their hearts. The President had to use all his moral power to restrain the violence. Lyndon Johnson sounded the call at Gettysburg for speedy Congressional action and for understanding and help from the average white citizen.

Governor Wallace chose this time for a dramatic confrontation with the federal government at the University of Alabama. This time, after trying the Federal Marshals, Kennedy immediately called up the Alabama National Guard, and Wallace backed down. But that same night, Medgar Evers, a field representative for the National Association for the Advancement of Colored People, one of the finest organizations working in the civil rights field, was shot in cold blood. Later, his alleged attacker was released by a Southern jury which said they couldn't reach a verdict!

In late August a peaceful March on Washington was proposed by Negro leader A. Philip Randolph, and this seemed to be the needed outlet for the pent-up frustration of the Civil Rights people. New space triumphs also took the mind of the nation off the immediate needs of the civil rights fight, and test ban talks with Russia took a turn for the better. For a time, there was a truce, but everyone knew that the summer of 1964 would come, and would be explosive.

In the midst of all the domestic unrest, President Kennedy fulfilled a promise to visit Germany. With Konrad Adenauer, he went to Mass at the historic Cathedral of Cologne and the crowds turned out in spontaneous welcome. In the serious talks that followed at Bonn, the Common Market, the stability of the dollar, and the future of a united Europe were discussed. Although Kennedy was the first American president born in the twentieth century, his vision was always on the future, the century to come. He was working to help found a whole new world order in which all men, at peace, could enjoy the results of a prosperous civilization and have the time and incentive to rise to new heights of human dignity.

Berliners poured out by the millions to chant "Ken-a-dee!" as he drove around the city. He went to the Berlin Wall and looked across to the desolate Communist area. The failure of Communism was never more obvious. Back at the City Hall he voiced these sentiments. "There are many people who don't understand—or say they don't understand—what the great issue is between the free world and the communist world. Let them come to Berlin. There are some who say that communism is the way of the future. Let them come to Berlin." Then, after saluting the spirit of freedom that was an example to the whole world, he cried out "Ich bin ein Berliner!" "I am a Berliner"—for anyone and everyone who fights for freedom knows that the front line of the battle is in Berlin.

Then he was off to Ireland to be greeted by more huge crowds chanting "Welcome Home." He visited his cousin Mary Ryan and stayed to have tea with her and her neighbors. He introduced two of his traveling companions, Dave Powers and Monsignor O'Mahoney, his Florida pastor. He became the first foreign head of state to speak in the Irish Parliament.

After a stop over in England to visit Prime Minister Macmillan, he flew on to Rome to visit the new pontiff, Pope Paul VI. One of the gifts given him by the Pope was a special copy of Pope John's encyclical *Pacem in Terris*. Pope John had been saving this for Kennedy, but died before he could bestow it. Pope John XXIII shared the same vision of the future that Kennedy had; their hearts and their spirit soared far beyond the limits of ordinary mortals.

When he returned home, he was met with news of an impending railroad strike, but he was also greeted by news from Moscow that Khrushchev was ready for a test ban treaty. In fact, Khrushchev had begun the talks with a joke—"Let's sign first and fill in the details later." Actually, the treaty was quickly arrived at, and after some short but formal debate, the Senate approved it. Kennedy went on TV to caution the nation about expecting too much from the treaty, yet it was a beginning, and, as he liked to point out, even a journey of a thousand miles must begin with the first step. The outraged cries of the right-wing extremists made it look like the treaty handed the country over to Moscow, but when the Senate finally voted, the vote was 80 for and 19 against.

All was not work for the President. He did take time out to try to teach some golf to Pierre Salinger, but it turned out to be something short of hopeless. Then, after the sadness of the death of Patrick Bouvier Kennedy, the crisis in Viet Nam blew wide open. The Diem regime had saved South Viet Nam from the Communists, but in the course of the years, it prospered on American military funds and lost touch with the people badly.

To complicate matters, the Diem family was intensely Catholic, and the Buddhist majority of the nation resented anything that looked like favoritism to Catholic generals or officials. Whether there was any truth to the charge or not, Diem and his family did nothing to counteract the charges, or even listen to them. Kennedy tried every means of persuasion in his power to get Diem to correct the situation, but to no avail. Finally, when a coup appeared possible, Kennedy decided to do nothing to encourage it, nothing to discourage it. He hoped the people of Viet Nam would solve their own internal problem and return, united, to the fight against Communism. The coup, inevitable when Diem proved intractable, did not bring any more unity to the nation and it did cause more headaches for the United States.

Kennedy felt that the people should hear about the peace and prosperity that his programs meant for them and for the world. He decided to use an old presidential device, "the non-political tour." In the three years of his term, the gross national product of the country, the index to national wealth, had grown by one hundred billion dollars and was growing faster than all of Europe and Russia put together. With facts like these to bring to the American people, Kennedy set out from Washington in late November to tell the people of the South. There was trouble in the Democratic party in Texas and JFK knew he would need that state in 1964, so with

Vice President Lyndon Johnson on one side of him and Governor Connolly on the other side, he went to the Lone Star State for the type of campaign tour he loved.

On the morning of November 22, 1963, the Kennedys appeared at a breakfast meeting in Fort Worth. Kennedy talked about the American space achievements and the responsibilities of citizenship. It had been a rainy morning, but as the motorcade formed, the sun came out and it promised to be a fine day. An aide carried the big Texas hat that had been given the President, since he made it a practice never to appear in the headgear that people always force upon candidates. Everyone wanted to see Jackie, and the photographers clustered around her. The women reporters discussed the color of her dress and decided it was raspberry pink. Larry O'Brien chatted with Senator Yarborough. It was a typical campaign swing.

At the Dallas airport over 5,000 people waited to get a wave or a handshake from the first family. The politicians smiled happily, for the tour was going better than could have been expected. The greatest concentration of right wing extremists existed in Southern California and in this part of Texas. Vice President Johnson and his Lady Bird had been jostled here, and UN Ambassador Adlai Stevenson had been roughed up here. But the crowds now were friendly, with only a bit of rancor evident at the fringes of the crowd. As the motorcade entered the downtown section of Dallas there were some signs of "Yankee go home" and even the bitter signs that showed the famous Kennedy profile and the big letters that spelled out "Wanted for Treason." But it was obvious that the crowds, the people, loved the President and his wife and they roared out their approval.

Then two shots rang out. JFK had just turned to wave, and he clutched at his throat. Governor Connolly pitched over. Jack Kennedy slumped against his wife. Then a third shot entered his brain. Jackie took one look and cried out, "They've killed my husband!" She turned back to get a Secret Service man into the car and then turned to cradle Jack's head against her breast. She was to be with him every minute after that, in the hospital, in the plane back to Washington, during the funeral and at the grave side in Arlington National Cemetery.

The car raced to the hospital, but the doctors knew at a glance that they had a dead president before them. Two priests who heard the bulletin on the radio dashed over to Parkland Memorial Hospital to anoint our fallen president. Their grief as they left the hospital told the nation the truth, a short time before the official bulletin was issued. After Father Huber had given the last Sacraments, Jackie bent over and slipped her wedding ring on the President's finger, an old Irish gesture of enduring love. On the trip to the hospital she had said over and over again, "Jack, I love you, I love you."

Her bloodstained clothes will be engraved on the memory of a whole generation of Americans who watched television that weekend. She stood by the new president as he was sworn in, a look of shocked dignity about her. Later she stepped off the plane in Washington and with Bob Kennedy's firm support, she accompanied the body to the White House. Her strength and her dignity, her grief and her bravery kept the whole nation from falling apart during those terrible four days. The nation recognized a valiant woman.

The wave of shock spread over the nation in a matter of minutes. The first news bulletins simply said that shots had been fired at the president's car. These were on the air by 12:33 P.M., Dallas time, three minutes after they rang out. Within another few minutes the news came that JFK had been hit. Then, all programs seemed to come to a halt, as the stations kept continuing coverage of the hospital watch. People wept openly on the streets; even reporters broke down as they made their announcements.

What had happened in Dallas? The first questions came—was it a right-wing plot, or Communists, or anti-Catholics? Anything seemed possible. Fast police work turned up the assassin and had him in custody less than two hours after he fired the shots.

Lee Harvey Oswald, an ex-Marine, an ex- Communist, a rebel aganst all society, stirred up by the climate of hate that right-wing extremists had spread in Dallas, was charged with the murder of the President. Months later the Warren Commission determined from the evidence that his deranged mind plotted and planned this alone, probably as a way of making his mark on history.

Sunday morning, another "loner," Jack Ruby shot and killed Oswald as millions watched on television. This wanton act only added to the tragedy of an emotion-filled weekend. For a time it seemed as if there would be no end to violence, no hope for future greatness.

World leaders immediately sent their expressions of grief. They came from Pope Paul VI and from Kings and Queens, from Presidents and Premiers, from the great and the little, all over the world. The people of America came in almost unending numbers to walk past the bier and pay their last respects. By Monday morning, world leaders and common citizens were forming in Washington to attend the funeral at St. Matthew's Cathedral.

Jacqueline, Caroline, little John were the center of the nation's sympathy. John saluted his father bravely as the coffin rolled by. Then Richard Cardinal Cushing led the nation in prayer as he celebrated the Requiem Mass. Finally, at Arlington National Cemetery Jackie lighted the eternal flame at the foot of the grave that was to be the symbol of the hopes that John Fitzgerald Kennedy had stirred in the nation at his Inauguration.

Millions of words have been written about these four days, and maybe as many pictures were taken. Still, the sense of loss cannot be told in print. President Johnson probably summed it up as simply and as effectively as human voice can do when he told Congress, "I would give anything I have and anything I own, not to be standing here today," and when he called upon the help of God that we might continue what John Kennedy had started.

For John Fitzgerald Kennedy had started the twenty-first century. He, along with Pope John XXIII, saw the turmoil of this generation as the death agony of the "modern" world and the birth pangs of a new civilization. The Renaissance, the reformation, and the industrial revolution marked new chapters in the history of the human race. They did not start on a certain single day, but they were the culmination of forces that grew within society. Dante, for instance, recognized the forces that were turning his world upside down, and he worked to channel those forces for the good of mankind. He is well called "the first modern man," but his century did not recognize him.

President Kennedy and Pope John understood that there were new vital forces struggling to be born in our time, and they tried to communicate that newness to us. The Catholic Church can no longer hide behind the security of medieval splendor, the traditions of an age long dead. The Church which drew up its magnificent defenses at the time of the Council of Trent must now go on a spiritual crusade to give meaning to life. The forces that St. Charles Borromeo and St. Robert Bellarmine directed to bring the good news of Christ to post-reformation Europe are as useless now as they were indispensable then, because Europe is a changed society. Life today is teeming with material progress; the Church must give this new life its meaning and direction.

This is exactly what John F. Kennedy saw. More scientific progress has been made in the last thirty years than in thirty centuries preceding our times. In God's Divine Providence, this is happening now, and since nothing happens without God's planning it, we must either accept these new responsibilities or return to barbarism. There is no alternative. We can live the new life or kill it—and where it is going we cannot clearly see. But Kennedy did not fear the future. If anything, he longed for it. This was the New Frontier that he foresaw, and he wanted his fellow Americans to rise to the challenge of the future. He wanted America to lead the way into the new civilization, to master it, to make it serve the human race, whatever it might turn out to be.

His bitter opponents were men of small minds and faint hearts, men who wanted to return to the supposed safety of the last century, men who feared their fellow men. When Pope John saw that the world trend toward socialism seemed inevitable, he proposed socialization, a channeling or a christening of that trend. He emphasized the voluntary union of free men to accomplish what otherwise will be done by blind, impersonal forces. When John Kennedy saw the needs of the human race demanding more united action, he proposed the extension and strengthening of true democratic processes so that free men might voluntarily direct their future. How similar were their ideals and goals! They drew their ideas from the same source—the Christian dignity of man.

When the nation mourned its president, some cried out bitterly, "Why did God let this happen?" But the real reaction should be, "Thank God that we were given men of such stature, for no matter how brief a time!" These two men renewed the spark of human hope and showed, in their own lives, what heights the man of the coming world can reach. Even their deaths were necessary, so that lesser men might dedicate themselves to the ideals for which Pope John and President Kennedy lived. With John Kennedy, America finally came of age in the world community of nations. Now it is necessary that we continue his work and his life. The ultimate betrayal would be to refuse to carry the torch that he lighted.

His individual works will quickly slip into their proper niche in history. They were the works that were called for by the necessities of our age, and they are no greater and no less than this age itself. The test ban treaty, the civil rights bill, the Alliance for Progress and the Peace Corps are facts to be labeled and catalogued and dated for the archives and the history books. The face-to-face stand with Communism may well be a real turning-point in history. But none of the things individually, nor the sum total of all of them, will give the true measure of John F. Kennedy. Not even his commitment to research marks him as any more than a well-informed statesman.

His vision and his ability to communicate that excitement of anticipation of the future are the keys to his personality and his greatness. He loved individual men, not mankind in general. He hated poverty and ignorance because they destroyed the spark of humanity in the individual. He fought for civil rights because he believed in human rights. And he believed in man, because he believed so firmly, so thoroughly, in God.

He worked for peace because he was not deceived by the shallow glow of glory that wartime bravery produces. He took the measure of a man not from the hair on his chest but from the strength of his heart and will. He urged his fellow citizens to be physically fit, not because he saw the strength of

JOHN F. KENNEDY, AMERICAN

a man in his muscles, but because a keen body becomes a better instrument for a good mind to use. He worked for a united world in which individual nations and individual men might work out their temporal and their eternal purposes. He wanted the best of both worlds for all men, insofar as is humanly possible, in real cooperation with God's plans.

This was John Fitzgerald Kennedy, American.

THE HOPE OF AN IDEALIST

THE FAITH OF A REALIST

THE COURAGE OF A PATRIOT

INTRODUCTION

It is both easy and difficult to write about President Kennedy. Easy, because his personality and his life were so colorful and challenging. Difficult, because he was so truly human that it is hard to give the whole picture. One can delve more deeply into the fascinating life of John Kennedy by examining for himself some of the speeches that the President made. JFK spoke from his heart. He communicated his goals and ideals, and these are part of his permanent legacy to mankind.

Included in this section are EXCERPTS *from various speeches which John Kennedy delivered during his term of office. These show the broad range of his interests and his love for every aspect of American life. They demonstrate the depth of his mind and the vast expanse of his vision. They prove that he had* THE HOPE OF AN IDEALIST, THE FAITH OF A REALIST AND THE COURAGE OF A REAL PATRIOT.

Our progress as a nation can be no swifter than our progress in education. Our requirements for world leadership, our hopes for economic growth, and the demands of citizenship itself in an era such at this, all require the maximum development of every young American's capacity.

The human mind is our fundamental resource.

A balanced Federal program must go well beyond incentives for investment in plant and equipment. It must include equally determined measures to invest in human beings, both in their basic education and training, and in their more advanced preparation for professional work. Without such measures, the Federal government will not be carrying out its responsibilities for expanding the base of our strength.

Education must remain a matter of state and local control, and higher education must remain a matter of individual choice. But education is increasingly expensive. Too many state and local governments lack the resources to assure an adequate education for every child. Too many classrooms are overcrowded. Too many teachers are underpaid. Too many talented individuals cannot afford the benefits of higher education. Too many academic institutions cannot afford the cost of, or find room for, the growing numbers of students seeking admission in the sixties.

Our twin goals must be: a new standard of excellence in education and the availability of such excellence to all who are willing and able to pursue it.

But an average net gain of nearly one million pupils a year during the next ten years will overburden a school system already strained by well over a half-million pupils in half-day sessions, a school system financed largely by a property tax incapable of bearing such an increased load in most communities.

These problems are common to all states. They are particularly severe in those states which lack the financial resources to provide a better education regardless of their own efforts. Additional difficulties, too often overlooked, are encountered in areas of special educational need. These areas include depressed areas and slum neighborhoods. The proportions of drop-outs, delinquency and classroom disorders in such areas is alarmingly high.

Therefore I recommend to Congress. . . .

The health of our nation is a key to the future—to its economic vitality, to the morale and efficiency of its citizens, to our success in achieving our own goals and in demonstrating to others the benefits of a free society. This is a matter of national concern.

More than twenty-five billion dollars a year, over six per cent of our national income, is being spent from public and private funds for health services. Yet there are major deficiencies in the quality and distribution of these services.

The dramatic results of new medicines and new methods, opening the way to a fuller and more useful life, are too often beyond the reach of those who need them most. Financial inability, absence of community resources and shortages of trained personnel keep too many people from getting what medical knowledge can obtain for them.

Those among us who are over sixty-five, sixteen million today in the United States, go to the hospital more often and stay longer than their younger neighbors. Their physical activity is limited by six times as much disability as the rest of the population. Their annual medical bill is twice that of persons under sixty-five, but their annual income is only half as high.

The nation's children, now forty per cent of our population, have urgent needs which must be met. Many still die in infancy. Many are not immunized against diseases which can be prevented, have inadequate diets, or unnecessarily endure physical and emotional problems.

These and other problems of health care can and must be met. Only a part of the responsibility rests with the Federal government. But its powers and resources make its role essential in four areas for improving health care: social insurance, facilities, personnel and research.

Twenty-six years ago this nation adopted the principles that every member of the labor force and his family should be insured against the haunting fear of loss of income caused by retirement, death and unemployment. To that we have added insurance against the economic loss caused by disability.

But there remains a significant gap that denies to all but those with the highest incomes a full measure of security: the high cost of ill health in old age. One out of five aged couples drawing Social Security benefits must go to the hospital each year. Half of those going to hospitals incur bills in excess of $700 a year. This is over one-third of their total annual income, more than a modest food budget for an entire year. Many simply do not obtain and cannot afford the care they need.

In our Social Security and Railroad Retirement systems we have the instruments which can spread the cost of health services in old age over the working years, effectively, and in a manner consistent with the dignity of the individuals. By using these proven systems to provide health insurance protection, it will be possible for our older people to get the vital hospital services they need without exhausting their vital resources or turning to public relief.

This self-supporting insurance method of financing the cost of such health services is certainly to be preferred to an expansion of public assistance, and should reduce the number of those needing medical care under the public relief program. The state and local money thus freed should be further used to help provide services not included in this proposal, and to assist those not covered.

In essence, I am recommending enactment of a health insurance program (Medicare) under the Social Security System. I propose that these insurance benefits be available to all persons aged sixty-five and over who are eligible for Social Security or Railroad Retirement benefits.

This program is not a program of socialized medicine. It is a program of prepayment of health costs with absolute freedom of choice guaranteed. Every person will choose his own doctor and hospital.

Latin America, Africa, the Middle East and Asia are caught up in the adventures of asserting their independence and modernizing their old ways of life. These new nations need aid in loans and technical assistance just as we in the northern half of the world drew successively on one another's capital and know-how as we moved into industrialization and regular growth.

But in our time these new nations need help for a special reason. Without exception they are under Communist pressure. In many cases, that pressure is direct and military. In others, it takes the form of intense subversive activity designed to break down and supersede the new, and often frail, modern institutions they have thus far built.

But the fundamental task of our foreign aid program in the 1960's is not negatively to fight Communism. Its fundamental task is to help make an historical demonstration that in the twentieth century as in the nineteenth, in the southern half of the globe as in the north, economic growth and political growth and political democracy can develop hand in hand.

In short, we have not only obligations to fulfill; we have great opportunities to realize. We are, I am convinced, on the threshold of a truly united and major effort by the free industrialized nations to assist the less-developed nations on a long-term basis.

JOHN F. KENNEDY, AMERICAN

Many of these less-developed nations are on the threshold of achieving sufficient economic, social and political strength and self-sustained growth to stand permanently on their own feet. The 1960's can be, and must be, the crucial "Decade of Development"; the period when many less-developed nations make the transition into self-sustained growth; the period in which an enlarged community of free, stable and self-reliant nations can reduce world tensions and insecurity.

This goal is in our grasp if, and only if, the other industrialized nations now join us in developing with the recipients a set of commonly agreed criteria, a set of long-range goals, and a common undertaking to meet these goals, in which each nation's contribution is related to the contributions of others and to the precise needs of each less-developed nation. Our job, in its largest sense, is to create a new partnership between the northern and southern halves of the world to which all free nations can contribute, in which each free nation must assume a responsibility proportional to its means.

We must unite the free industrialized nations in a common effort to help those nations within reach of stable growth get under way. The foundation for this unity has already been laid by the creation of the Organization for Economic Co-operation and Development under the leadership of President Eisenhower. Such a unified effort will help launch the economies of the newly developing countries "into orbit," bringing them to a stage of self-sustained growth where extraordinary outside assistance is not required. If this can be done, and I have every reason to hope it can be done, then this decade will be a significant one indeed in the history of free men.

But our success in achieving these goals, in creating an environment in which the energies of struggling peoples can be devoted to constructive purposes in the world community, and our success in enlisting a greater common effort toward this end on the part of other industrialized nations, depends to a large extent upon the scope and continuity of our own efforts. If we encourage recipients to dramatize a series of short-term crises as a basis for our aid, instead of depending on a plan for long-term goals, then we will dissipate our funds, our good will and our leadership. Nor will we be any nearer either to our security goals or to the end of the foreign aid burden.

In short, this Congress at this session must make possible a dramatic turning point in this troubled history of foreign aid to the underdeveloped world. We must say to the less-developed nations, if they are willing to undertake necessary internal reform and self-help, and to the other industrialized nations, if they are willing to undertake a much greater effort on a much broader scale, that we then intend during this coming decade of development to achieve a decisive turn-around in the fate of the less-developed world, looking toward the ultimate day when all nations can be self-reliant and when foreign aid will no longer be needed.

The vast task of economic development urgently requires skilled people to do the work of the society; to help teach in the schools, construct development projects, demonstrate modern methods of sanitation in the villages, and perform a hundred other tasks calling for training and advanced knowledge.

To meet this urgent need for skilled manpower we are proposing the establishment of a Peace Corps, an organization which will recruit and train American volunteers, sending them abroad to work with the people of other nations.

This organization will differ from existing assistance programs in that its members will supplement technical advisers by offering the specific skills needed by developing nations if they are to put technical advice to work. They will help provide the skilled manpower necessary to carry out the development projects planned by the host governments, acting at a working level and serving at great personal sacrifice. There is little doubt that the number of those who wish to serve will be far greater than our capacity to absorb them. . . .

Most heartening of all, the initial reaction to this proposal has been an enthusiastic response by student groups, professional organizations and private citizens everywhere, a convincing demonstration that we have in this country an immense reservoir of dedicated men and women willing to devote their energies and time and toil to the cause of world peace and human progress.

Among the specific programs to which Peace Corps members can contribute are: teaching in primary and secondary schools, especially as part of national English-language-teaching programs; participation in the world-wide program of malaria eradication; instruction and operation of public health and sanitation projects; aiding in village development through school construction and other programs; increasing rural agricultural productivity by assisting local farmers to use modern implements and techniques. The initial emphasis of these programs will be on teaching. . . .

The Peace Corps will not be limited to the young or to college graduates. All Americans who are qualified will be welcome to join this effort. But undoubtedly the Corps will be made up primarily of young people as they complete their formal education.

Because one of the greatest resources of a free society is the strength and diversity of its private organizations and institutions, much of the Peace Corps program will be carried out by these groups, financially assisted by the Federal Government.

Peace Corps personnel will be made available to developing nations in the following ways:

1. Through private voluntary agencies carrying on international assistance programs.

2. Through overseas programs of colleges and universities.

3. Through assistance programs of international agencies.

4. Through assistance programs of the United States Government.

5. Through new programs which the Peace Corps itself directly administers. . . .

In all instances the men and women of the Peace Corps will go only to those countries where their services and skills are genuinely needed and desired. . . .

The people of Latin America are the inheritors of a deep belief in political democracy and the freedom of man, a sincere faith that the best road to progress is freedom's road. But if the Act of Bogotá becomes just another empty declaration, if we are unwilling to commit our resources and energy to the task of social progress and economic development, then we face a grave and imminent danger that desperate peoples will turn to Communism or other forms of tyranny as their only hope for change. Well-organized, skillful and strongly financed forces are constantly urging them to take this course.

A few statistics will illustrate the depth of the problems of Latin America. This is the fastest-growing area in the world. Its current population of 195 million represents an increase of about 30 per cent over the past ten years, and by the 1980's the continent will have to support more than 400 million people. At the same time the average per capita annual product is only $280, less than one-ninth that of the United States; and in large areas, inhabited by millions of people, it is less than $70. Thus it is a difficult task merely to keep living standards from falling further as population grows.

Such poverty inevitably takes its toll in human life. The average American can expect to live seventy years, but life expectancy in Latin America is only forty-six, dropping to about thirty-five in some Central American countries. And while our rate of infant mortality is less than 30 per thousand, it is more than 110 per thousand in Latin America.

Perhaps the greatest stimulus to our own development was the establishment of universal basic education. But for most of the children of Latin America education is a remote and unattainable dream. Illiteracy extends to almost half the adults, reaching 90 per cent in one country. And approximately 50 per cent of school-age children have no schools to attend.

In one major Latin-American capital a third of the total population is living in filthy and unbearable slums. In another country 80 percent of the entire population is housed in makeshift shacks and barracks, lacking the privacy of separate rooms for families.

It was to meet these shocking and urgent conditions that the Act of Bogotá was signed. This Act, building on the concept of Operation Pan America initiated by Brazil in 1958, introduced two important new elements to the efforts to improve living standards in South America.

First, the nations of Latin America have recognized the need for an intensive program of self-help: mobilizing their domestic resources, and undertaking basic reforms in tax structure, in land ownership and use, and in education, health and housing.

Second, it launches a major inter-American program for the social progress which is an indispensable condition to growth, a program for improved land use, education, health and housing.

9. *Kennedy, American*

Let it be clear—and this is a judgment which the Members of Congress must finally make—let it be clear that I am asking the Congress and the country to accept a firm commitment to a new course which will last for many years and carry very heavy costs of $531 million in fiscal 1962, an estimated $7 billion to $9 billion additional over the next five years. If we are to go only halfway, or reduce our sights in the face of difficulty, in my judgment it would be better not to go at all.

Now this is a choice which this country must make, and I am confident that under the leadership of the Space Committees of the Congress and the Appropriating Committees, you will consider the matter carefully.

It is a most important decision that we make as a nation. But all of you have lived through the last four years and have seen the significance of space and the adventures in space, and no one can predict with certainty what the ultimate meaning will be of mastery of space.

I believe we should go to the moon. But I think every citizen of this country as well as the Members of the Congress should consider the matter carefully in making their judgment, to which we have given attention over many weeks and months, because it is a heavy burden, and there is no sense in agreeing or desiring that the United States take an affirmative position in outer space, unless we are prepared to do the work and bear the burdens to make it successful. If we are not, we should decide today. . . .

This decision demands a major national commitment of scientific and technical manpower, material and facilities, and the possibility of their diversion from other important activities where they are already thinly spread. It means a degree of dedication, organization and discipline which have not always characterized our research and development efforts. It means we cannot afford undue work stoppages, inflated costs of material or talent, wasteful interagency rivalries, or a high turnover of key personnel.

New objectives and new money cannot solve these problems. They could, in fact, aggravate them further, unless every scientist, every engineer, every serviceman, every technician, contractor and civil servant gives his personal pledge that this nation will move forward, with the full speed of freedom, in the exciting adventure of space.

COMMUNISM: (*Meeting with Khrushchev*)
JUNE 6, 1961

I wanted to present our views to him directly, precisely, realistically, and with an opportunity for discussion and clarification. This was done. No new aims were stated in private that have not been stated in public on either side. The gap between us was not, in such a short period, materially reduced, but at least the channels of communication were opened more fully, at least the chances of a dangerous misjudgment on either side should now be less, and at least the men on whose decisions the peace in part depends have agreed to remain in contact.

This is important, for neither of us tried merely to please the other, to agree merely to be agreeable, to say what the other wanted to hear, and just as our judicial system relies on witnesses appearing in court and on cross-examination instead of hearsay testimony or affidavits on paper, so too, was this direct give-and-take of immeasurable value in making clear and precise what we considered to be vital, for the facts of the matter are that the Soviets and ourselves give wholly different meanings to the same words—war, peace, democracy and popular will.

We have wholly different views of right and wrong, of what is an internal affair and what is aggression, and above all, we have wholly different concepts of where the world is and where it is going.

196   JOHN F. KENNEDY, AMERICAN

Only by such a discussion was it possible for me to be sure that Mr. Khrushchev knew how differently we view the present and the future. Our views contrasted sharply but at least we knew better at the end where we both stood. Neither of us was there to dictate a settlement or convert the other to a cause or to concede our basic interests. But both of us were there, I think, because we realized that each nation has the power to inflict enormous damage upon the other, that such a war could and should be avoided if at all possible since it would settle no dispute and prove no doctrine, and that care should thus be taken to prevent our conflicting interests from so directly confronting each other that war necessarily ensued.

We believe in a system of national freedom and independence. He believes in an expanding and dynamic concept of world Communism, and the question was whether these two systems can ever hope to live in peace without permitting any loss of security or any denial of freedom of our friends. However difficult it may seem to answer this question in the affirmative as we approach so many harsh tests, I think we owe it to all mankind to make every possible effort.

This is why I consider the Vienna talks useful. The somber mood that they conveyed was not cause for elation or relaxation, nor was it cause for undue pessimism or fear. It simply demonstrated how much work we in the free world have to do and how long and hard a struggle must be our fate as Americans in this generation as the chief defenders of the cause of liberty.

The program to be presented to this Assembly, for general and complete disarmament under effective international control, moves to bridge the gap between those who insist on a gradual approach and those who talk only of the final and total achievement. It would create machinery to keep the peace as it destroys the machines of war. It would proceed through balanced and safeguarded stages designed to give no state a military advantage over another. It would place the final responsibility for verification and control where it belongs, not with the big powers alone, not with one's adversary or one's self, but in an international organization within the framework of the United Nations.

It would assure that indispensable condition of disarmament, true inspection, in stages proportionate to the stage of disarmament. It would cover delivery systems as well as weapons. It would ultimately halt their production as well as their testing, their transfer as well as their possession. It would achieve, under the eye of an international disarmament organization, a steady reduction in forces, both nuclear and conventional, until it had abolished all armies and all weapons except those needed for internal order and a new United Nations Peace Force. And it starts that process now, today, even as the talks begin.

In short, general and complete disarmament must no longer be a mere slogan, used to resist the first steps. It is no longer to be a goal without means of achieving it, without means of verifying its progress, without means of keeping the peace. It is now a realistic plan, and a test, a test of those only willing to talk and those willing to act.

Such a plan would not bring a world free from conflict or greed, but it would bring a world free from the terrors of mass destruction. It would not usher in the era of the super-state, but it would usher in an era in which no state could annihilate or be annihilated by another.

In 1945, this nation proposed the Baruch plan to internationalize the atom before other nations even possessed the bomb or demobilized their troops. We proposed with allies the Disarmament Plan of 1951 while still at war in Korea. And we make our proposals today, while building up our defenses over Berlin, not because we are inconsistent or insincere or intimidated, but because we know the rights of free men will prevail, because while we are compelled against our will to rearm, we look confidently beyond Berlin to the kind of disarmed world we all prefer.

I therefore propose, on the basis of this plan, that disarmament negotiations resume promptly, and continue without interruption until an entire program for complete and general disarmament has not only been agreed upon but actually achieved.

JOHN F. KENNEDY, AMERICAN

A strong America depends on its cities, America's glory and sometimes America's shame. To substitute sunlight for congestion and progress for decay, we have stepped up existing urban renewal and housing programs, and launched new ones; redoubled the attack on water pollution; speeded aid to airports, hospitals, highways and our declining mass transit systems; and secured new weapons to combat organized crime, racketeering and youth delinquency, assisted by the coordinated and hard-hitting efforts of our investigative services; the FBI, the Internal Revenue, the Bureau of Narcotics and many others. We shall need further anti-crime, mass transit and transportation legislation, and new tools to fight air pollution. And with all this effort under way, both equity and common sense require that our nation's urban areas, containing three-fourths of our population, sit as equals at the Cabinet table. I urge a new Department of Urban Affairs and Housing.

A strong America also depends on its farms and natural resources. American farmers took heart in 1961, from a billion-dollar rise in farm income and from a hopeful start on reducing the farm surpluses. But we are still operating under a patchwork accumulation of old laws, which cost us $1 billion a year in CCC carrying charges alone, yet fail to halt rural poverty or boost farming earnings.

Our task is to master and turn to fully fruitful ends the magnificent productivity of our farms and farmers. The revolution on our own countryside stands in the sharpest contrast to the repeated farm failures of the Communist nations and is a source of pride to us all. Since 1950 our agricultural output per man-hour has actually doubled! Without new, realistic measures, it will someday swamp our farmers and our taxpayers in a national scandal or a farm depression.

I will therefore submit to the Congress a new comprehensive farm program, tailored to fit the use of our land and the supplies of each crop to the long-range needs of the sixties, and designed to prevent chaos in the sixties with a program of common sense.

We also need for the sixties, if we are to bequeath our full national estate to our heirs, a new, long-range conservation and recreation program expansion of our superb national parks and forests, preservation of our authentic wilderness areas, new starts on water and power projects as our population steadily increases, and expanded REA generation and transmission loans.

But America stands for progress in human rights as well as economic affairs, and a strong America requires the assurance of full and equal rights to all its citizens, of any race or any color. This administration has shown as never before how much could be done through the full use of Executive powers, through the enforcement of laws already passed by the Congress, through persuasion, negotiation and litigation, to secure the constitutional rights of all: the right to vote, the right to travel without hindrance across state lines, and the right to free public education.

I issued last March a comprehensive order to guarantee the right to equal employment opportunity in all federal agencies and contractors. The Vice President's Committee thus created has done much, including the voluntary "Plans for Progress" which, in all sections of the country, are achieving a quiet but striking success in opening up to all races new professional, supervisory and other job opportunities.

But there is much more to be done—by the Executive, by the courts and by the Congress. Among the bills now pending before you, on which the Executive departments will comment in detail, are appropriate methods of strengthening these basic rights which have our full support. The right to vote, for example, should no longer be denied through such arbitrary devices on a local level, sometimes abused, such as literacy tests and poll taxes. As we approach the one hundredth anniversary, next January, of the Emancipation Proclamation, let the acts of every branch of the government, and every citizen, portray that "righteousness does exalt a nation."

The Charter of Punta del Este, which last August established the Alliance for Progress, is the framework of goals and conditions for what has been called "a peaceful revolution on a hemispheric scale."

That revolution had begun before the Charter was drawn. It will continue after its goals are reached. If its goals are not achieved, the revolution will continue, but its methods and results will be tragically different. History has removed for governments the margin of safety between the peaceful revolution and the violent revolution. The luxury of a leisurely interval is no longer available.

These were the facts recognized at Punta del Este. These were the facts that dictated the terms of the Charter. And these are the facts which require our participation in this massive cooperative effort.

✻ ✻ ✻

During the year beginning last March over one billion dollars has been committed in Latin America by the United States in support of the Alliance, fulfilling the pledge we made at the first Punta del Este meeting, and launching in a very real way for this hemisphere a dramatic Decade of Development. But even with this impressive support, the destiny of the Alliance lies largely in the hands of the countries themselves. For even large amounts of external aid can do no more than provide the margin which enables each country through its own determination and action to achieve lasting success.

The United States recognized that it takes time to develop careful programs for national development and the administrative capacity necessary to carry out such a program to go beyond the enactment of land reform measures and actually transfer the land and make the most productive use of it, to pass new tax laws and then achieve their acceptance and enforcement. It is heartening, therefore, that the changes called for by the Alliance for Progress have been the central issue in several Latin-American elections, demonstrating that its effects will be deep and real. Under the Organization of American States, nine outstanding economists and development advisers have begun to assist countries in critically reviewing their plans.

Three Latin-American countries have already completed and submitted for review their plans for the more effective mobilization of their resources toward national development. The others are creating and strengthening their mechanisms for development planning. A number of Latin-American countries have already taken significant steps toward land or tax reform; and throughout the region there is a new ferment of activity, centered on improvements in education, in rural development, in public administration and on other essential institutional measures required to give a sound basis for economic growth.

But more important still is the changed attitudes of peoples and governments already noticeable in Latin America. The Alliance has fired the imagination and kindled the hopes of millions of our good neighbors. Their drive toward modernization is gaining momentum as it unleashes the energies of these millions; and the United States is becoming increasingly identified in the minds of the people with the goal they move toward: a better life with freedom. Our hand, extended in help, is being accepted without loss of dignity.

But the Alliance is barely under way. It is a task for a decade, not for a year.

There is no strife, no prejudice, no national conflict in outer space as yet. Its hazards are hostile to us all. Its conquest deserves the best of all mankind, and its opportunity for peaceful cooperation may never come again. But why, some say, the moon? Why choose this as our goal? And they may well ask, why climb the highest mountain? Why, thirty-five years ago, fly the Atlantic? Why does Rice play Texas?

We choose to go to the moon. We choose to go to the moon in this decade, and do the other things, not because they are easy but because they are hard; because that goal will serve to organize and measure the best of our energies and skills; because that challenge is one that we are willing to accept, one we are unwilling to postpone, and one which we intend to win—and the others, too.

It is for these reasons that I regard the decision last year to shift our efforts in space from low to high gear as among the most important decisions that will be made during my incumbency in the office of the Presidency.

In the last twenty-four hours we have seen facilities now being created for the greatest and most complex exploration in man's history. We have felt the ground shake and the air shattered by the testing of a Saturn C-1 booster rocket, many times as powerful as the Atlas which launched John Glenn, generating power equivalent to ten thousand automobiles with their accelerators on the floor. We have seen the site where five F-1 rocket engines, each one as powerful as all eight engines of the Saturn combined, will be clustered together to make the advanced Saturn missile, assembled in a new building to be built at Cape Canaveral as tall as a forty-eight-story structure, as wide as a city block and as long as two lengths of this field.

Within these last nineteen months at least forty-five satellites have circled the earth. Some forty of them were "made in the United States of America," and they were far more sophisticated and supplied far more knowledge to the people of the world than those of the Soviet Union.

The Mariner spacecraft now on its way to Venus is the most intricate instrument in the history of space science. The accuracy of that shot is comparable to firing a missile from Cape Canaveral and dropping it in this stadium between the forty-yard lines.

Transit satellites are helping our ships at sea to steer a safer course. Tiros satellites have given us unprecedented warnings of hurricanes and storms, and will do the same for forest fires and icebergs.

We have had our failures, but so have others, even if they do not admit them. And they may be less public.

To be sure, we are behind, and will be behind for some time in manned flight. But we do not intend to stay behind, and in this decade we shall make up and move ahead.

The growth of our science and education will be enriched by new knowledge of our universe and environment, by new techniques of learning and mapping and observation, by new tools and computers for industry, medicine, the home as well as the school. Technical institutions, such as Rice, will reap the harvest of these gains.

And finally, the space effort itself, while still in its infancy, has already created a great number of new companies and tens of thousands of new jobs. Space and related industries are generating new demands in investment and skilled personnel, and this city and this state and this region will share greatly in this growth. What was once the farthest outpost on the new frontier of science and space, Houston, your city of Houston, with its Manned Spacecraft Center, will become the heart of a large scientific and engineering community. During the next five years the National Aeronautics and Space Administration expects to double the number of scientists and engineers in this area, to increase its outlays for salaries and expenses to $60 million a year, to invest some $200 million in plant and laboratory facilities, and to direct or contract for new space efforts over $1 billion from this center in this city.

To be sure, all this costs us all a good deal of money; this year's space budget is three times what it was in January, 1961, and it is greater than the space budget of the previous eight years combined. That budget now stands at $5.4 billion a year—a staggering sum, though somewhat less than we pay for cigarettes and cigars every year. Space expenditures will soon rise some more, from forty cents per person per week to more than fifty cents a week for every man, woman and child in the United States, for we have given this program a high national priority—even though I realize that this is in some measure an act of faith and vision, for we do not now know what benefits await us.

Nevertheless, it is hard for any nation to focus on an external or subversive threat to its independence when its energies are drained in daily combat with the forces of poverty and despair. It makes little sense for us to assail, in speeches and resolutions, the horrors of Communism, to spend $50 billion a year to prevent a military advance, and then to begrudge spending, largely on American products, less than one-tenth of that amount to help other nations strengthen their independence and cure the social chaos in which Communism has always thrived.

I am proud, and I think most Americans are proud, of a mutual defense and assistance program, evolved with bipartisan support in three administrations, which has, with all of its recognized problems, contributed to the fact that not a single one of the nearly fifty United Nations members to gain independence since the Second World War has succumbed to Communist control.

I am proud of a program and of a country that has helped to arm and feed and clothe millions of people who live on the front lines of freedom. I am especially proud that this country has put forward for the sixties a vast cooperative effort to achieve economic growth and social progress throughout the Americas—the Alliance for Progress.

I do not underestimate the difficulties that we face in this mutual effort among our close neighbors, but the free states of this hemisphere, working in close collaboration, have begun to make this Alliance a reality. Today it is feeding one out of every four school-age children in Latin America an extra food ration from our farm surpluses. It has distributed 1.5 million schoolbooks and is building 17,000 classrooms. It has helped resettle tens of thousands of farm families on land they can call their own. It is stimulating our good neighbors to more self-help and reform—fiscal, social, institutional and land reforms. It is bringing housing and hope and health to millions who were forgotten. The men and women of this hemisphere know that the Alliance cannot succeed if it is only another name for United States handouts, that it can succeed only as the Latin American nations themselves devote their best efforts of fulfilling its goals.

This story is the same in Africa, in the Middle East and in Asia. Wherever nations are willing to help themselves, we stand ready to help them build new bulwarks of freedom. We are not purchasing votes for the Cold War; we have gone to the aid of imperiled nations, neutrals and allies alike. What we do ask, and all that we ask, is that our help be used to the best advantage, and that their own efforts not be diverted by needless quarrels with other independent nations.

Despite all its past achievements, the continued progress of the Mutual Assistance Program requires a persistent discontent with present progress. We have been organizing this program to make it a more effective and efficient instrument, and that process will continue this year.

But free world development will still be an uphill struggle. Governmental aid can only supplement the role of private investment, trade expansion, commodity stabilization and, above all, internal self-improvement. The processes of growth are gradual, bearing fruit in a decade, not a day. Our successes will be neither quick nor dramatic. But if these programs were ever to be ended, our failures in a dozen countries would be sudden and would be certain.

Neither money nor technical assistance, however, can be our only weapon against poverty. In the end, the crucial effort is one of purpose, requiring the fuel of finance and also a torch of idealism. And nothing carries the spirit of this American idealism and expresses our hopes better and more effectively to the far corners of the earth than the American Peace Corps.

A year ago less than nine hundred Peace Corps volunteers were on the job. A year from now they will number more than nine thousand—men and women, aged eighteen to seventy-nine, willing to give two years of their lives to helping people in other lands. There are, in fact, nearly one million

Americans serving their country and the cause of freedom in overseas posts, a record no other people can match.

Surely those of us who stay at home should be glad to help indirectly, by supporting our aid programs; by opening our doors to foreign visitors and diplomats and students; and by proving, day by day, by deed as well as by word, that we are a just and generous people.

There is an especially urgent need for college level training of technicians to assist scientists, engineers and doctors. Although ideally one scientist or engineer should have the backing of two or three technicians, our institutions today are not producing even one technician for each three science and engineering graduates. This shortage results in an inefficient use of professional manpower—the occupation of critically needed time and talent to perform tasks which could be performed by others—an extravagance which cannot be tolerated when the nation's demand for scientists, engineers and doctors continues to grow. Failure to give attention to this matter will impede the objectives of the graduate and postgraduate training programs mentioned below. I recommend, therefore, a program of grants to aid public and private nonprofit institutions in the training of scientific, engineering and medical technicians in two-year college-level programs, covering up to 50 percent of the cost of constructing and equipping as well as operating the necessary academic facilities.

Special urgency exists for expanding the capacity for the graduate training of engineers, scientists and mathematicians. The President's Science Advisory Committee has recently reported that an unprecedented acceleration in the production of advanced degrees is immediately necessary to increase our national capability in these fields. Added facilities, larger faculties and new institutions are needed. I have recommended, therefore, in the proposed 1964 budget already before the Congress, a strengthening of the National Science Foundation matching grant program for institutions of higher education to expand and improve graduate and undergraduate science facilities.

Because today's trend in colleges and universities is toward less lecturing and more independent study, the college and university library becomes even more essential in the life of our students. Today, as reported by the American Library Association, nearly all college libraries are urgently in need of additional books, periodicals, scientific number of students and faculty. Additionally, they need buildings, equipment and publications to serve their academic communities, whether public or private. I recommend the authorization of federal grants to institutions of higher education for library materials and construction, on a broad geographic basis, with priority to those most urgently requiring expansion and improvement.

Expansion of high-quality graduate education and research in all fields is essential to national security and economic growth. Means of increasing our supply of highly trained professional personnel to match the rapidly growing demands of teaching, industry, government and research warrants our interest and support.

"There are few earthly things more beautiful than a university," wrote John Masefield, in his tribute to the English universities, and his words are equally true here. He did not refer to spires and towers, to campus greens and ivied walls. He admired the splendid beauty of the university, he said, because it was "a place where those who hate ignorance may strive to know, where those who perceive truth may strive to make others see."

I have therefore chosen this time and this place to discuss a topic on which ignorance too often abounds and the truth is too rarely perceived, yet it is the most important topic on earth: world peace.

What kind of peace do I mean? What kind of peace do we seek? Not a Pax Americana enforced on the world by American weapons of war. Not the peace of the grave or the security of the slave. I am talking about genuine peace, the kind of peace that makes life on earth worth living, the kind that enables men and nations to grow and to hope and to build a better life for their children—not merely peace for Americans, but peace for all men and women; not merely peace in our time, but peace for all time.

I speak of peace because of the new face of war. Total war makes no sense in an age when great powers can maintain large and relatively invulnerable nuclear forces and refuse to surrender without resort to those forces. It makes no sense in an age when a single nuclear weapon contains almost ten times the explosive force delivered by all the Allied air forces in the Second World War. It makes no sense in an age when the deadly poisons produced by a nuclear exchange would be carried by the wind and water and soil and seed to the far corners of the globe and to generations yet unborn.

Today the expenditure of billions of dollars every year on weapons acquired for the purpose of making sure we never need to use them is essential to keeping the peace. But surely the acquisition of such idle stockpiles, which can only destroy and never create, is not the only, much less the most efficient, means of assuring peace.

I speak of peace, therefore, as the necessary rational end of rational men. I realize that the pursuit of peace is not as dramatic as the pursuit of war, and frequently the words of the pursuer fall on deaf ears. But we have no more urgent task.

* * *

Let us focus instead on a more practical, more attainable peace, based not on a sudden revolution in human nature but on a gradual evolution in human institutions, on a series of concrete actions and effective agreements which are in the interest of all concerned. There is no single, simple key to this peace, no grand or magic formula to be adopted by one or two powers. Genuine peace must be the product of many nations, the sum of many acts. It

JOHN F. KENNEDY, AMERICAN

must be dynamic, not static, changing to meet the challenge of each new generation. For peace is a process, a way of solving problems.

With such a peace there will still be quarrels and conflicting interests, as there are within families and nations. World peace, like community peace, does not require that each man love his neighbor; it requires only that they live together in mutual tolerance, submitting their disputes to a just and peaceful settlement. And history teaches us that enmities between nations, as between individuals, do not last forever. However fixed our likes and dislikes may seem, the tide of times and events will often bring surprising changes in relations between nations and neighbors.

So let us persevere. Peace need not be impracticable, and war need not be inevitable. By defining our goal more clearly, by making it seem more manageable and less remote, we can help all peoples to see it, to draw hope from it, and to move irresistibly toward it.

❅ ❅ ❅

No Government or social system is so evil that its people must be considered as lacking in virtue. As Americans we find Communism profoundly repugnant as a negation of personal freedom and dignity. But we can still hail the Russian people for their many achievements—in science and space, in economic and industrial growth, in culture and in acts of courage.

Among the many traits the peoples of our two countries have in common, none is stronger than our mutual abhorrence of war. Almost unique among the major world powers, we have never been at war with each other. And no nation in the history of battle ever suffered more than the Soviet Union suffered in the course of the Second World War. At least twenty million lost their lives. Countless millions of homes and farms were burned or sacked. A third of the nation's territory, including nearly two-thirds of its industrial base, was turned into a wasteland—a loss equivalent to the devastation of this country east of Chicago.

Today, should total war ever break out again, no matter how, our two countries would become the primary targets. It is an ironical but accurate fact that the two strongest powers are the two in the most danger of devastation. All we have built, all we have worked for, would be destroyed in the first twenty-four hours. And even in the Cold War, which brings burdens and dangers to so many countries, including this nation's closest allies, our two countries bear the heaviest burdens. For we are both devoting massive sums of money to weapons that could be better devoted to combating ignorance, poverty and disease. We are both caught up in a vicious and dangerous cycle in which suspicion on one side breeds suspicion on the other and new weapons beget counterweapons.

JOHN F. KENNEDY, AMERICAN

In short, both the United States and its allies, and the Soviet Union and its allies, have a mutually deep interest in a just and genuine peace and in halting the arms race. Agreements to this end are in the interests of the Soviet Union as well as ours, and even the most hostile nations can be relied upon to accept and keep those treaty obligations, and only those treaty obligations, which are in their own interest.

So let us not be blind to our differences, but let us also direct attention to our common interests and to the means by which those differences can be resolved. And if we cannot end now our differences, at least we can help make the world safe for diversity. For in the final analysis our most basic common link is that we all inhabit this planet. We all breathe the same air. We all cherish our children's future. And we are all mortal.

We must, therefore, persevere in the search for peace, in the hope that constructive changes within the Communist bloc might bring within reach solutions which now seem beyond us. We must conduct our affairs in such a way that it becomes in the Communists' interest to agree on a genuine peace. Above all, while defending our own vital interests, nuclear powers must avert those confrontations which bring an adversary to a choice of either a humiliating retreat or a nuclear war. To adopt that kind of course in the nuclear age would be evidence only of the bankruptcy of our policy or of a collective death wish for the world.

To secure such ends, America's weapons are nonprovocative, carefully controlled, designed to deter and capable selective use. Our military forces are committed to peace and disciplined in self-restraint. Our diplomats are instructed to avoid unnecessary irritants and purely rhetorical hostility.

For we seek a relaxation of tensions without relaxing our guard. And, for our part, we do not need to use threats to prove that we are resolute. We do not need to jam foreign broadcasts out of fear our faith will be eroded. We are unwilling to impose our system on any unwilling people, but we are willing and able to engage in peaceful competition with any people on earth.

Meanwhile we seek to strengthen the United Nations, to help solve its financial problems, to make it a more effective instrument of peace, to develop it into a genuine world security system—a system capable of resolving disputes on the basis of law, of insuring the security of the large and the small, and of creating conditions under which arms can finally be abolished.

CIVIL RIGHTS: JUNE 11, 1963

This afternoon, following a series of threats and defiant statements, the presence of Alabama National Guardsmen was required at the University of Alabama to carry out the final and unequivocal order of the United States District Court of the Northern District of Alabama. That order called for the admission of two clearly qualified young Alabama residents who happened to have been born Negro.

That they were admitted peacefully on the campus is due in good measure to the conduct of the students of the University of Alabama, who met their responsibilities in a constructive way.

I hope that every American, regardless of where he lives, will stop and examine his conscience about this and other related incidents. This nation was founded by men of many nations and backgrounds. It was founded on the principle that all men are created equal, and that the rights of every man are diminished when the rights of one man are threatened.

Today we are committed to a world-wide struggle to promote and protect the rights of all who wish to be free, and when Americans are sent to Vietnam or West Berlin, we do not ask for whites only. It ought to be possible, therefore, for American students of any color to attend any public institution they select without having to be backed up by troops.

It ought to be possible for American consumers of any color to receive equal service in places of public accommodation, such as hotels and restaurants and theaters and retail stores, without being forced to resort to demonstrations in the street, and it ought to be possible for American citizens of any color to register and to vote in a free election without interference or fear of reprisal.

It ought to be possible, in short, for every American to enjoy the privileges of being American without regard to his race or his color. In short, every American ought to have the right to be treated as he would wish to be treated, as one would wish his children to be treated. But this is not the case.

The Negro baby born in America today, regardless of the section of the nation in which he is born, has about one-half as much chance of completing high school as a white baby born in the same place on the same day, one-third as much chance of completing college, one-third as much chance of becoming a professional man, twice as much chance of becoming unemployed, about one-seventh as much chance of earning $10,000 a year, a life expectancy which is seven years shorter, and the prospect of earning only half as much.

This is not a sectional issue. Difficulties over segregation and discrimination exist in every city, in every state of the Union, producing in many cities a rising tide of discontent that threatens the public safety. Nor is this a partisan issue in a time of domestic crisis. Men of good will and generosity should be able to unite regardless of party or politics. This is not even a legal or legislative issue alone. It is better to settle these matters in the courts than on the streets, and new laws are needed at every level, but law alone cannot make men see right.

We are confronted primarily with a moral issue. It is as old as the Scriptures and is as clear as the American Constitution.

The heart of the question is whether all Americans are to be afforded equal rights and equal opportunities, whether we are going to treat our fellow Americans as we want to be treated. If an American, because he is dark, cannot eat lunch in a restaurant open to the public, if he cannot send his children to the best public school available, if he cannot vote for the public officials who represent him, if, in short, he cannot enjoy the full and free life which all of us want, then who among us would be content to have the color of his skin changed and stand in his place? Who among us would then be content with the counsels of patience and delay?

Secret violations are possible and secret preparations for a sudden withdrawal are possible, and thus our own vigilance and strength must be maintained, as we remain ready to withdraw and to resume all forms of testing if we must. But it would be a mistake to assume that this treaty will be quickly broken. The gains of illegal testing are obviously slight compared to their cost and the hazard of discovery, and the nations which have initialed and will sign this treaty prefer it, in my judgment, to unrestricted testing as a matter of their own self-interest, for these nations, too and all nations, have a stake in limiting the arms race, in holding the spread of nuclear weapons and in breathing air that is not radioactive. While it may be theoretically possible to demonstrate the risks inherent in any treaty—and such risks in this treaty are small—the far greater risks are to our security of unrestricted testing, the risk of a nuclear arms race, the risk of new nuclear powers, nuclear pollution and nuclear war.

This limited test ban, in our most careful judgment, is safer by far for the United States than an unlimited nuclear arms race. For all these reasons, I am hopeful that this nation will promptly approve the limited test ban treaty. There will, of course, be debate in the country and in the Senate. The Constitution wisely requires the advice and consent of the Senate to all treaties, and that consultation has already begun. All this is as it should be A document which may mark an historic and constructive opportunity for the world deserves an historic and constructive debate.

It is my hope that all of you will take part in that debate, for this treaty is for all of us. It is particularly for our children and our grandchildren, and they have no lobby here in Washington. This debate will involve military, scientific and political experts, but it must not be left to them alone. The right and the responsibility are yours.

If we are to open new doorways to peace, if we are to seize this rare opportunity for progress, if we are to be as bold and farsighted in our control of weapons as we have been in their invention, then let us now show all the world on this side of the wall and the other that a strong America also stands for peace.

There is no cause for complacency. We have learned in times past that the spirit of one moment or place can be gone in the next. We have been disappointed more than once, and we have no illusions now that there are short cuts on the road to peace. At many points around the globe the Communists are continuing their efforts to exploit weakness and poverty. Their concentration of nuclear and conventional arms must still be deterred.

The familiar contest between choice and coercion, the familiar places of danger and conflict, are still therein in Cuba, in Southeast Asia, in Berlin and all around the globe, still requiring all the strength and the vigilance that we can muster. Nothing could more greatly damage our cause than if we and our allies were to believe that peace has already been achieved and that our strength and unity were no longer required.

But now, for the first time in many years, the path of peace may be open. No one can be certain what the future will bring. No one can say whether the time has come for an easing of the struggle. But history and our own conscience will judge us more harshly if we do not now make every effort to test our hopes by action, and this is the place to begin. According to the ancient Chinese proverb, "A journey of a thousand miles must begin with a single step."

My fellow Americans, let us take that first step. Let us, if we can, get back from the shadows of war and seek out the way of peace. And if that journey is one thousand miles, or even more, let history record that we, in this land, took the first step.

The provision of development assistance by individual nations must go on. But the United Nations also must play a larger role in helping bring to all men the fruits of modern science and industry. A United Nations conference on this subject held earlier this year at Geneva opened new vistas for the developing countries. Next year a United Nations Conference on Trade will consider the needs of these nations for new markets. And more than four-fifths of the entire United Nations system can be found today mobilizing the weapons of science and technology for the United Nations' Decade of Development.

But more can be done.

A world center for health communications under the World Health Organization could warn of epidemics and the adverse effects of certain drugs, as well as transmit the results of new experiments and new discoveries.

Regional research centers could advance our common medical knowledge and train new scientists and doctors for new nations.

A global system of satellites could provide communication and weather information for all corners of the earth.

A world-wide program of conservation could protect the forest and wild game preserves now in danger of extinction for all time, improve the marine harvest of food from our oceans, and prevent the contamination of air and water by industrial as well as nuclear pollution.

And, finally, a world-wide program of farm productivity and food distribution, similar to our country's "Food for Peace" program, could now give every child the food he needs.

But man does not live by bread alone, and members of this organization are committed by the Charter to promote and respect human rights. Those rights are not respected when a Buddhist priest is driven from his pagoda, when a synagogue is shut down, when a Protestant church cannot open a mission, when a cardinal is forced into hiding or when a crowded church service is bombed. The United States of America is opposed to discrimination and persecution on grounds of race and religion anywhere in the world, including our own nation. We are working to right the wrongs of our own country.

Through legislation and administrative action, through moral and legal commitment, this government has launched a determined effort to rid our nation of discrimination which has existed too long—in education, in housing, in transportation, in employment, in the Civil Service, in recreation and in places of public accommodation. And therefore, in this or any other forum, we do not hesitate to condemn racial or religious injustice, whether committed or permitted by friend or foe.

I know that some of you experienced discrimination in this country. But I ask you to believe me when I tell you that this is not the wish of most Americans, that we share your regret and resentment, and that we intend to end such practices for all time to come, not only for our visitors but for our citizens as well.

I hope that not only our nation but all other multiracial societies will meet these standards of fairness and justice. We are opposed to apartheid and all forms of human oppression. We do not advocate the rights of black Africans in order to drive out white Africans. Our concern is the right of all men to equal protection under the law; and since human rights are indivisible, this body cannot stand aside when those rights are abused and neglected by any member state.

New efforts are needed if this Assembly's Declaration of Human Rights, now fifteen years old, is to have full meaning. And new means should be found for promoting the free expression and trade of ideas, through travel and communication, and through increased exchanges of people and books and broadcasts. For as the world renounces the competition of weapons, competition in ideas must flourish, and that competition must be as full and as fair as possible.

The United States delegation will be prepared to suggest to the United Nations initiatives in the pursuit of all the goals. For this is an organization for peace, and peace cannot come without work and progress.

* * *

The United Nations cannot survive as a static organization. Its obligations are increasing as well as its size. Its charter must be changed as well as its customs. The authors of that charter did not intend that it be frozen in perpetuity. The science of weapons and war has made us all, far more than eighteen years ago in San Francisco, one world and one human race, with one common destiny. In such a world absolute sovereignty no longer assures us of absolute security. The conventions of peace must pull abreast and then ahead of the inventions of war. The United Nations, building on its successes and learning from its failures, must be developed into a genuine world security system.

But peace does not rest in charters and covenants alone. It lies in the hearts and minds of all people. And in this world no act, no pact, no treaty, no organization can hope to preserve it without the support and the wholehearted commitment of all people. So let us not rest all our hopes on parchment and on paper. Let us strive to build peace, a desire for peace, a willingness to work for peace, in the hearts and minds of all of our people. I believe that we can. I believe the problems of human destiny are not beyond the reach of human beings.

JOHN F. KENNEDY, AMERICAN

Two years ago I told this body that the United States had proposed, and was willing to sign, a limited test ban treaty. Today that treaty has been signed. It will not put an end to war. It will not remove basic conflicts. It will not secure freedom for all. But it can be a lever, and Archimedes, explaining the principles of the lever, was said to have declared to his friends: "Give me a place where I can stand, and I shall move the world."

My fellow inhabitants of this planet, let us take our stand here in this Assembly of nations. And let us see if we, in our own time, can move the world to a just and lasting peace.

As I said recently at the United Nations, even little wars are dangerous in this nuclear world. The long labor of peace is an undertaking for every nation, large and small, for every member of the Family of Man. "In this effort none of us remain unaligned. To this goal none can be uncommitted." If the Family of Man cannot achieve greater unity and harmony, the very planet which serves as its home may find its future in peril.

But there are other troubles besetting the human family. Many of its members live in poverty and misery and despair. More than one out of three, according to the FAO, suffer from malnutrition or undernutrition or both—while more than one in ten live below the breadline. Two out of every five adults on this planet are, according to UNESCO, illiterate. One out of eight suffers from trachoma or lives in an area where malaria is still a clear and present danger. Ten million—nearly as many men, women and children as inhabit this city and Los Angeles combined—still suffer from leprosy; and countless others suffer from yaws or tuberculosis or intestinal parasites.

For the blessings of life have not been distributed evenly to the Family of Man. Life expectancy in this most fortunate of nations has reached the Biblical three score years and ten; but in the less developed nations of Africa, Asia and Latin America, the overwhelming majority of infants cannot expect to live even two score years and five. In those vast continents, more than half the children of primary school age are not in school. More than half the families live in substandard dwellings. More than half the people live on less than $100 a year. Two out of every three adults are illiterate.

The Family of Man can survive differences of race and religion. Contrary to the assertions of Mr. Khrushchev, it can accept differences of ideology, politics and economics. But it cannot survive in the form in which we know it of nuclear war—and neither can it long endure the growing gulf between the rich and the poor.

The rich must help the poor. The industrialized nations must help the developing nations. And the United States, along with its allies, must do better—not worse—by its foreign aid program, which is now being subjected to such intensive debate in the Senate of the United States.

Too often we advance the need to foreign aid only in terms of our economic self-interest. To be sure, foreign aid is in our economic self-interest. It provides more than a half a million jobs for workers in every state. It finances a rising share of our exports and builds new and growing export markets. It generates the purchase of military and civilian equipment by other governments in this country. It makes possible the stationing of 3½ million troops along the Communist periphery at a price one-tenth the cost of maintaining a comparable number of American soldiers. And it helps to stave off the kind of chaos or Communist takeover or Communist attack that would surely demand our critical and costly attention.

* * *

Nearly two years ago my wife and I visited Bogotá, Colombia, where a vast new Alliance for Progress housing project was just getting under way. Earlier this year I received a letter from the first resident of this 1,200-new-house development. "Now," he wrote, "we have dignity and liberty."

Dignity and liberty—these words are the foundation, as they have been since 1947, of the mutual security program. For the dignity and liberty of all free men, of a world of diversity where the balance of power is clearly on the side of free nations, is essential to the security of the United States. And to weaken and water down the pending program, to confuse and confine its flexibility with rigid restrictions and rejections, will not only harm our economy; it will hamper security. It will waste our present investment and it will, above all, forfeit our obligations to our fellow man, obligations that stem from our wealth and strength, from our devotion to freedom and from our membership in the Family of Man.

* * *

Some say that they are tiring of this task. We are tired of world problems and their complexities.

We are tired of hearing those who receive our aid disagree with us. But are we tired of living in a free world? Do we expect that world overnight to be like the United States? Are we going to stop now merely because we have not produced complete success?

I do not believe our adversaries are tired, and I cannot believe that the United States of America in 1963 is fatigued.

Surely the Americans of the 1960's can do half as well as the Americans of the 1950's. Surely we are not going to throw away our hopes and means for peaceful progress in an outburst of irritation and frustration. I do not want it said of us what T. S. Eliot said of others some years ago: "These were a decent people. Their only monument: the asphalt road and a thousand lost golf balls."

I think we can do better than that.

My fellow Americans, I hope we will be guided by our interests. I hope we will recognize that the struggle is by no means over; that it is essential that we not only maintain our effort but that we also persevere; that we not only endure, in Mr. Faulkner's words, but also prevail. It is essential, in short, that the word go forth from the United States to all who are concerned about the future of the Family of Man that we are not weary in well-doing. And I am confident, if we maintain the pace, we shall in due season reap the kind of world we deserve and deserve the kind of world we shall have.

The first and most frequently asked question is: Is the federal government growing so large that our private economy is endangered? My answer to that is no. The federal government has been growing for 175 years. Our population has grown even faster. Our territory and economy have grown and become more closely linked. The size of our business, labor, farm and other establishments and organizations has increased. Above all, our responsibilities around the world have grown and our stake in world peace has grown immeasurably. Life itself is more complex and the American people in the twentieth century have come to expect more from governmental action. But there has been no sudden spurt in the growth of government under this administration.

Leaving national security outlays aside, the federal civilian expenditures today, when measured as they should be measured in a growing economy as a percentage of our national output, are no higher than they were at the end of the Second World War—a mere 5 percent of our Gross National Product is not a threat to our economy. The real growth in government has been at the state and local level. Between 1948 and 1962, while federal civilian expenditures were rising by 65 percent, state spending, on the average, across this country rose by 227 percent—from less than $10 billion in 1948 to over $30 billion in 1962. Florida's state expenditures in that same period rose by 270 percent, or more than four times as fast, percentagewise, as the federal budget; Georgia by 331 percent; Ohio by 300 percent; Kentucky by 431 percent.

The federal government has no desire to expand the size and scope of its activities merely for the sake of expansion. Many tasks would never have been taken on by the Congress had they been able to be fulfilled at the state and local level, and this administration has made efforts to transfer to private ownership many of the financial assets held by the government, to substitute private for public credit, to reduce farm surpluses, to dispose of excess commodities and to make our transportation system less restrictive. This is a far cry, I believe, from a government too big for the economy.

Secondly, I am asked: Are not continuing deficits and the mounting national debt certain to drive us into bankruptcy? And my answer to that is no. Once again we must look at these facts in perspective. From 1948 to 1962 the total federal debt increased less than 20 percent. We had the Korean War, all our obligations abroad, a tremendously growing country, tremendously growing population. The federal debt grew by less than 20 percent, while the average for all the states was 500 percent. Or, taking only the four years from 1958 to 1962, the federal debt rose only 8 percent, while state debt as a whole went up 41 percent.

Obviously, neither the states nor the nation are teetering on the edge of bankruptcy as the result of these debts. In 1945 our national debt was 120 percent of our Gross National Product. Today it is 53 percent. Next year it will be 52 percent. At a time when our debt has gone up by the percentage I described, our Gross National Product has doubled and, therefore, as this country moves to a trillion dollar economy, which we are moving toward, it is quite obvious that as long as we maintain these proportions the fiscal credit of the United States will still be secure.

While the federal net debt was growing less than 20 percent in these years, total corporate debt—not mine, your debt—was growing by nearly 200 percent and the total indebtedness of private individuals rose by 300 percent. So who is the most cautious fiscal manager, you gentlemen or us?

THE LAST SPEECH: DALLAS, NOV. 22, 1963

I have spoken of strength largely in terms of the deterrence and resistance of aggression and attack. But, in today's world, freedom can be lost without a shot being fired, by ballots as well as bullets. The success of our leadership is dependent upon respect for our mission in the world as well as our missiles—on a clearer recognition of the virtues of freedom as well as the evils of tyranny.

That is why our Information Agency has doubled the short-wave broadcasting power of the Voice of America and increased the number of broadcasting hours by 30 percent, increased Spanish language broadcasting to Cuba and Latin America from one to nine hours a day, increased sevenfold to more than 3.5 million copies the number of American books being translated and published for Latin-American readers, and taken a host of other steps to carry our message of truth and freedom to all the far corners of the earth.

And that is also why we have regained the initiative in the exploration of outer space, making an annual effort greater than the combined total of all space activities undertaken during the fifties, launching more than 130 vehicles into earth orbit, putting into actual operation valuable weather and communications satellites, and making it clear to all that the United States of America has no intention of finishing second in space.

This effort is expensive, but it pays its own way, for freedom and for America. For there is no longer any fear in the free world that a Communist lead in space will become a permanent assertion of supremacy and the basis of military superiority. There is no longer any doubt about the strength and skill of American science, American industry, American education and the American free enterprise system. In short, our national space effort represents a great gain in, and a great resource of, our national strength—and both Texas and Texans are contributing greatly to this strength.

Finally, it should be clear by now that a nation can be no stronger abroad than she is at home. Only an America which practices what it preaches about equal rights and social justice will be respected by those whose choice affects our future. Only an America which has fully educated its citizens is fully capable of tackling the complex problems and perceiving the hidden dangers of the world in which we live. And only an America which is growing and prospering economically can sustain the world-wide defenses of freedom, while demonstrating to all concerned the opportunities of our system and society.

It is clear, therefore, that we are strengthening our security as well as our economy by our recent record increases in national income and output—by surging ahead of most of Western Europe in the rate of business expansion and the margin of corporate profits, by maintaining a more stable level of prices than almost any of our overseas competitors, and by cutting personal and corporate income taxes by some $11 billion, as I have proposed, to assure this nation of the longest and strongest expansion in our peacetime economic history.

This nation's total output—which three years ago was at the $500 billion mark—will soon pass $600 billion, for a record rise of over $100 billion in three short years. For the first time in history we have 70 million men and women at work. For the first time in history average factory earnings have exceeded $100 a week. For the first time in history corporation profits after taxes—which have risen 43 percent in less than three years—have reached an annual level of $27.4 billion.

My friends and fellow citizens, I cite these facts and figures to make it clear that America today is stronger than ever before. Our adversaries have not abandoned their ambitions; our dangers have not diminished; our vigilance cannot be relaxed. But now we have the military, the scientific and the economic strength to do whatever must be done for the preservation and promotion of freedom.

That strength will never be used in pursuit of aggressive ambitions; it will always be used in pursuit of peace. It will never be used to promote provocations; it will always be used to promote the peaceful settlement of disputes.

We in this country, in this generation, are, by destiny rather than choice, the watchmen on the walls of world freedom.

We ask, therefore, that we may be worthy of our power and responsibility, that we may exercise our strength with wisdom and restraint, and that we may achieve in our time and for all time the ancient vision of "peace on earth, good will toward men." That must always be our goal—and the righteousness of our cause must always underlie our strength. For as was written long ago: "Except the Lord keep the city, the watchman watcheth but in vain."

DAUGHTERS OF ST. PAUL

IN MASSACHUSETTS
  50 St. Paul's Ave.
    Jamaica Plain
    Boston, Mass. 02130
  172 Tremont St.
    Boston, Mass. 02111
  381 Dorchester St.
    So. Boston, Mass. 02127
  325 Main St.
    Fitchburg, Mass.
IN NEW YORK
  78 Fort Place
    Staten Island, N.Y. 10301
  625 East 187th St.
    Bronx, N.Y.
  39 Erie St.
    Buffalo, N.Y. 14202
IN CONNECTICUT
  202 Fairfield Ave.
    Bridgeport, Conn. 06603
IN OHIO
  141 West Rayen Ave.
    Youngstown, Ohio 44503
  Daughters of St. Paul
    Cleveland, Ohio
IN TEXAS
  114 East Main Plaza
    San Antonio, Texas 78205
IN CALIFORNIA
  1570 Fifth Ave.
    San Diego, Calif. 92101
  278 - 17th Street
    Oakland, California 94612
IN LOUISIANA
  86 Bolton Ave.
    Alexandria, La. 71301
IN FLORIDA
  2700 Biscayne Blvd.
    Miami, Florida 33137
IN CANADA
  8885 Blvd. Lacordaire
    St. Leonard Deport-Maurice
    Montreal, Canada
      1063 St. Clair Ave. West
    Toronto, Canada
IN ENGLAND
  29 Beauchamp Place
    London, S.W. 3, England
IN AFRICA
  Box 4392
    Kampala, Uganda
IN INDIA
  Water Field Road Extension
  Plot No. 143
    Bandra, India
IN THE PHILIPPINE ISLANDS
  2650 F.B. Harrison St.
  Pasay City
    Philippine Islands
IN AUSTRALIA
  58 Abbotsford Rd.
    Homebush N.S.W., Australia
  226 Victoria Square
    Adelaide, South-Australia
  6 Muir Street
    Hawthorn, Victoria, Australia